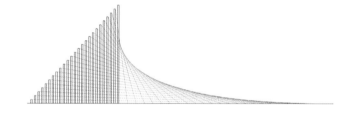

MATERIALIZING THE IMMATERIAL

THE ARCHITECTURE OF WALLACE CUNNINGHAM

MATERIALIZING THE IMMATERIAL

THE ARCHITECTURE OF WALLACE CUNNINGHAM

by Joseph Giovannini

Preface by Sam Maloof

YALE UNIVERSITY

Distributed by Yale University Press

New Haven and London

Published by Yale University

© 2006 by Yale University

Available through Yale University Press

P.O. Box 209040, New Haven, Connecticut 06520-9040

ISBN: 0-9749565-2-x

All rights reserved. This book may not be reproduced, in whole or in part, including illustrations, in any form (beyond that copying permitted by Section 107 and 108 of the U.S. Copyright Law and except by reviewers for the public press), without written permission from the publishers.

The paper in this book meets the guidelines for permanance and durability of the Committee on Production Guidelines for Book Longevity of the Council on Library Resources.

Printed in China by C & C Printing Co. Ltd.

10 9 8 7 6 5 4 3 2

PHOTOGRAPHY CREDITS

Kerry Bauer: 149 (left), 150 (top), 151 (bottom right)

Wallace Cunningham: Cover image, 2-3, 6-7, 8-9, 10, 15, 16, 18 (right), 19, 21, 23, 24 (all), 25 (all), 32, 36, 37, 38, 43 (top), 46, 47, 52, 53 (model), 56, 57, 59 (right), 60, 61, 63 (all), 67, 71, 72-73, 76 (all), 77, 78, 80, 81, 84 (right), 89, 90, 91 (middle), 91 (right), 99, 100, 106 (left), 107 (all), 110, 113, 115 (right), 116 (left), 117 (all), 118-119, 120-121, 122, 124, 125, 126 (all), 127, 128 (all), 129 (left), 129 (middle), 131, 132-133 (site), 144 (left), 144 (middle), 146 (right), 147 (top middle), 147 (bottom middle), 147 (bottom right), 148 (right), 151 (top), 151 (bottom middle), 154 (all), 155 (all), back cover image.

Jeff Divine: 48, 49

Dr. and Mrs. Dean Eastman: 20

Ed Gohlich: 45 (bottom), 150 (bottom left)

Geoffrey Uhl 153

William Guillette: 39, 40 (top left), 134, 142, 143, 148 (left), 150 (bottom middle), 151 (bottom left), 153 (bottom left)

David Hewitt/Anne Garrison: 14, 51, 55, 70, 76 (left), 123, 129 (right), 153 (bottom middle)

Joan Hix-VanderSchuit: 40 (bottom right), 42, 45 (top), 50 (all), 64, 65 (all), 150 (bottom right)

Chuck LaChiusa: 17 right

Stephen Mangione: 12–13, 16 left

John Oswald: 44

Erhard Pfeiffer: 29, 33, 34, 35, 66, 68, 69, 75, 82, 83, 84 (left), 85, 88, 91 (left), 92, 94, 95, 96-97, 101, 102, 103, 104-105, 106 (right), 108, 112, 114, 116(right), 146 (left), 146 (middle)

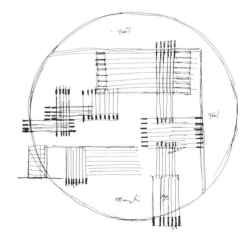

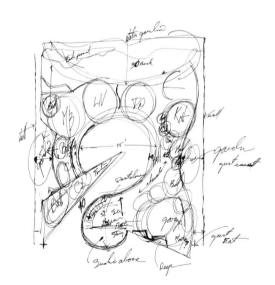

ACKNOWLEDGMENTS

Wallace Cunningham wishes to thank Arthur and Alice Kramer for making this publication possible.

Joseph Giovannini • Lori Stein

Frances Snow Moran • Mary Snow • Faith Hawkins

Marya Lilien • Ling Po

Pamela Smith, my wife of 20 years, for her love, devotion, and art direction.

Guy West and Peggy Walther without whom most of this work simply would not have been possible.

Julie Divine • Geoffrey Uhl • Carol Carlson

Julianne Griffin, John Donatich, and the rest of the Yale University Press staff.

Architectural Digest/Conde Nast, specifically Paige Rense, James Huntington, and Jeffrey Nemeroff for the use of their photographs, direction, and making a success of my work.

It takes a community of builders, artisans, engineers, landscape architects, installers, lighting technicians, engineering consultants, environmentalists to produce structures and environments. Most of all it is the clients who provide opportunities for us to express ourselves. Without them we would all be frustrated.

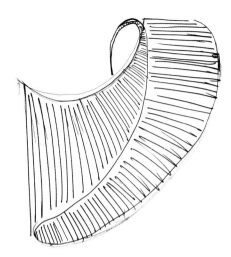

CAPTIONS FOR PAGES 1-7

Page 1: *Chapel elevation*

Pages 2–3: *Beamwork over the walled garden at Harmony*

Pages 4–5: *Sketches (left to right) of Voler, Crescent, Ray, and Seascape*

Pages 6–7: *Stepped perimeter wall at Razor Bluff*

Designed by Areta Buk, Thumbprint Design

Production by Lori Stein, Layla Productions, Inc.

Wallace Cunningham, self-taught in architecture except for a few months at Taliesin West, is a free spirit. I believe he travels in a creative realm that only a few can ever enter. In my sixty years of designing and making furniture, I have been fortunate to work with many designers and architects. How excited I felt when I saw Cunningham's 1995 Saltman house. Here was a beautiful piece of sculpture that one could live in! I was asked to do some pieces for it—a privilege and a challenge, and the beginning of our good friendship. Wally's work continues to amaze and astound. He is a true genius—a master of light, space, and design.

SAM MALOOF
WOODWORKER

Razor Bluff's swimming pool in the foreground, with its infinity edge merging into the ocean beyond.

My approach to design is more intuitive than intellectual, but I always strive for an architecture of clarity and rigor. I begin with a catalyst, which can be as simple as a distinctive site feature or as complex as a client's extraordinary desire. I react to this catalyst by instinct in hopes that the process will yield a design with spirit and emotion.

Spirituality and emotion are integral to my work. I try to tap into the psyche with unexpected manipulations of form and light, which are intended to be as sculptural as they are architectural. Natural light is a crucial element in my designs and is used to define, fragment, and animate space. The environment is a primary source of inspiration and a driving force as well. Nature is not static, nor should be the efforts of man. Dealing with spaces as solids in a design causes the building to become extremely confined, static, and without spirit. Open up a structure to sky, landscape, and view and the building becomes alive. Your soul has a place to enter.

WALLACE E. CUNNINGHAM

Left and right: *The courtyard and surrounding roof shapes, made of white Portland cement, at Razor Bluff, looking skyward, during construction.*

CHAPTER 1

SHADOW AND LIGHT

Enchanted spaces occur rarely in any culture, and their appearance is especially infrequent in secular societies. Although American suburbia has been a venue of much experimental architecture since the late nineteenth century, especially in Southern California, architects designing for the suburban lot have seldom addressed the possibility of mystifying space in the domestic sphere, at the scale of a house.

But on a quintessentially suburban street of single-family houses, in the cultural shadow of Louis Kahn's Salk Institute, San Diego architect Wallace Cunningham designed a house with an evocative stillness comparable not only to the Salk but also to religious edifices whose spaces over the centuries cultivated the spiritual. On an affluent but otherwise unremarkable block, Cunningham, however, achieves in his design of Brushstroke, the Barbara and Paul Saltman residence, a spatial spirituality without the religion.

Seen from the curb, high, simple, sinuously curved walls define an inner precinct in which Cunningham has located a black paisley-shaped swimming pool. The architect builds the pool up from the ground, and detaches it on one side from the outer pale gray walls so that the entire basin is freestanding. Water brims to edges designed to disappear, and the black contours of the water play off the curves of the outer walls fencing the yard, all under the canopy of feathery pines outside. The walls, which mask the street,

cloister the space with a quiet that allows the shifting patterns of light and shadow to register clearly on the abstract architectural surfaces. Breezes ripple across the black water.

There is a physics to spatial enchantment, and the designer mastered this physical and visual science at Brushstroke. Cunningham created a precinct of tranquillity with the boundary walls, establishing conditions necessary for the visual amplification of the atmospheric ephemera that are normally lost in unprotected, visually competitive spaces. Then he introduced the content of the meditation: the water, its unfathomable blackness, and walls that anticipate the shadows and shifting coloration of the western light projected by the setting sun. He set up the space as a receptacle for phenomena that the environment itself will set into play.

Cunningham isolated his interest in the potential aura of space over many years spent observing the qualities of buildings that moved him. During a highly individualistic practice, much of it as a self-educated solo practitioner, he cultivated the architectural skills that allowed him to control the environment so that the materials of construction

Preceding pages: *Grain elevators along waterfront in Buffalo, New York.* Left and right: *Light and shadow accent the swimming pool and a curved wall at Brushstroke.*

themselves, and the architectural detail, would support ambitious aesthetic goals predicated on the fragility of fugitive environmental effects. Cunningham, whose formal education was sporadic and never culminated in a degree

Above: *The Darwin Martin House in Buffalo (1904-1906, Frank Lloyd Wright, architect).*
Above right: *Elaborate terracotta decoration on Buffalo's Prudential (formerly Guaranty) Building (1895-1896, Adler and Sullivan, architects). The building's surface contributes to its meaning.*

or an architectural license, was certainly influenced by many architects and even schools of thought. But the influences fell on an unusual talent. Inside Brushstroke, its owner displays a collection of fine Asian antiques she and her husband collected over a lifetime. But among them is a small pile of pyramidal wood blocks cut off from the corners of the many doors fitted into the house's special geometries. About a dozen pieces form the angular clusters, and each grouping is a spontaneous work of art—ingeniously fitted, beautifully formed, structurally stable, visually dynamic. The groupings frequently change because

Cunningham often drops in to visit his client, and the house. He sculpts new groupings as he visits.

Cunningham is an unusual case. In the late 1950s and early '60s, he grew up one of nine children in a three-bedroom apartment in a working-class neighborhood of Buffalo, New York, situated between grain elevators and oil refineries. Cunningham was one of five brothers who bunked in a single bedroom, the dressers stacked. Only one room was heated. His father worked at Bethlehem Steel; his mother was an artistically sensitive woman who practiced calligraphy and played the piano, often in local

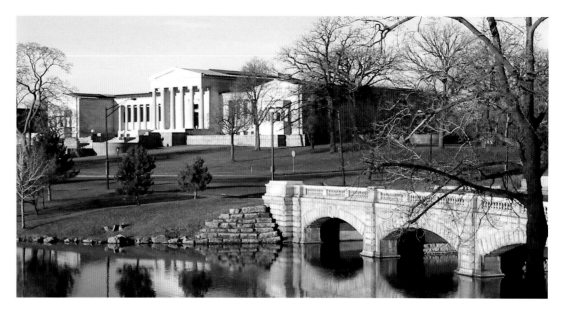

churches. At thirteen, Cunningham took his first job, bottling chlorine for pools.

If the material struggle was accompanied by the psychological tension of deep poverty and, in the Cunningham household, the added distress of erratic par-

Above left: *Buffalo's South Park Conservatory (1898, Lord and Burnham Company, architects); based on the Joseph Paxton's Crystal Palace in London.*
Above right: *The Albright-Knox Art Gallery (1900-1905, Green and Wicks, architects), based on a Greek temple.*

enting, Buffalo offered Cunningham a culturally supportive context with a rare architectural patrimony that resonated with his emerging sensibility. An affluent canal city and regional capital in the late-nineteenth and early-twentieth centuries, Buffalo commissioned buildings and landscape plans by H. H. Richardson, Daniel Burnham, Louis Sullivan, Frederick Law Olmsted, and Frank Lloyd Wright, and later by Eliel and Eero Saarinen and Gordon Bunshaft. The Cunningham house itself was located near Wright's Larkin Building, though the building was already demolished by the time Wallace was growing up.

Cunningham's mother introduced him to notable buildings on their cultural outings, including Wright's magisterial Martin House. He remembers Wright's book *The Natural House* (which a brother had checked out from the library) for the architect's attention to detail and for his design philosophy. "The Martin House is the first Wright house I actually saw. I was about twelve, and I'd never realized that this other life existed. I loved the way it took control of the property. The house was heavy and dark, but then these ribbons of light came through into the rooms, and some of the spaces, like the side porch,

made this transition between the house and garden: It was a generous outside room thrust into the garden, with a roof, floor, and furniture but without the windows."

Architecture for the young man in a culturally motivated but materially deprived home environment was a revelation. "My mom was artistic, but there was no purpose, no structure to it. She was an ethereal artist. Here was art that served a purpose, that was more than just intellectual or beautiful in the abstract."

At a distance, the city offered visions of architecture that registered on his young psyche. These glimpses into cultural worlds outside his immediate family orbit would typify what he calls the "little tiny bits of education" that characterized his episodic formation as an architect until he would finally set up practice in San Diego in his mid twenties. "There was nothing beautiful about my childhood, and the Martin house, and houses I'd see later that also had its haunting, religious quality, must have had something to do with the search in my practice for beauty and order." Many, like Brushstroke, seem like comforting retreats into absolute tranquillity.

His mother died when Cunningham was sixteen, after which the older children cared for the younger ones: Wallace found himself responsible for three siblings. But at eighteen, after briefly attending Hutchinson Technical High School for Architecture and then graduating from South

Park High School, Cunningham availed himself of the family's own "underground" railroad to Chicago, and he moved in with an older sister living there, as other siblings had done before. His sister lived in Aurora, Illinois, a town with an island in its river, impressive bridges with statues, and numerous buildings by the distinguished Chicago firm Purcell and Elmslie.

His intellectual biography as an adult starts in 1973 when, during a drive up the Fox River Valley in the far Chicago suburbs, he and his sister chanced on a Prairie-Style house that echoed the Martin House, and Cunningham decided to knock on the door. Occupied by Frances Snow Moran and Mary Snow, the house was indeed by Wright, and the two were daughters of the couple who had since 1910 owned the residence, known as Wright's Gridley House. The sisters ran an antiques

Far left: *Buffalo's City Hall (1929-1931, George J. Dietel and John J. Wade, with Sullivan J. Jones, architects), one of the great Art Deco monuments in America, refers to ideological, historical, and artistic movements from antiquity through modern times.* Left: *The Snow residence, also known as The Gridley House, in Batavia, Illinois (1906, Frank Lloyd Wright, architect).* Right: *Kleinhans Music Hall (1938-1940, Eliel and Eero Saarinen with F. J. and W. A. Kidd, architects).*

store on the ground floor, and they hired Cunningham as a handyman. Soon enough he was living in the butler's quarters in the back of the five-acre property, plastering cracks and finishing furniture in a house caught, according to Cunningham, "in suspended decay."

The Snows knew owners of other Wright houses, and through a friend, were invited to visit the Coonley House in Riverside, Illinois. Built in 1911–12, the house is one of Wright's greatest, a *gesamtkunstwerk* down to the lighting fixtures and the leaded abstractions of branches in the windows. With the Japanese quality of its low roof and its perfect proportions, Cunningham admired the house for what he calls its "religious quality": "It really spoke: haunt-

ing, beautiful, mysterious. I didn't want to leave. In other Wright houses, such as the Gridley House, you know what to expect, but in Coonley, you had to explore it to understand. You couldn't get it quickly."

The young man had fallen into a circle of bluestockings with a network that extended to Chicago academia and ultimately to Taliesin. The Snow sisters felt Cunningham needed to continue his education, and they introduced him to friends at the Chicago Academy of Fine Arts, where he enrolled in the fall of 1974, on a scholarship partially funded by the Snows. Cunningham would spend three semesters at the Academy in what would prove a formative period that conditioned him to look at the world

through an ultimately interdisciplinary framework blurring art and architecture. Ruth Van Sickle Ford, the Academy's founder, had commissioned Bruce Goff to design the Ford House in Aurora. Marya de Czarnecka Lilien, a Polish architect and aristocrat who had headed the Department of Interior Architecture at the School of The Art Institute of Chicago, taught architecture history at the Academy, and proved an inspirational mentor who introduced Cunningham to the work of such figures as John Lautner. Cunningham also studied photography, sculpture, and printmaking at the Academy, establishing the basis of an artistic sensibility that he would later apply to architecture, and of an armature of learning through the arts.

Mary Snow introduced young Cunningham to Virgil Gilman, director of the Fox Valley Park District, who hired the student as a curator responsible for Americana in the park's museum. There he designed displays and exhibitions, and became involved with the preservation and restoration of several historic structures, including a log cabin and train station. While at the Fox Valley museum, the student designed his first structure, a wedge-shaped seating deck dramatically cantilevered out toward the Fox River, made of recycled oak slats, with rounded contours wrapping an extruded profile. Cunningham had no formal architectural training when he designed and executed this clean-lined, sophisticated structure.

De Czarnecka Lilien, who lectured on Wright, was an honored apprentice at Taliesin, and during Cunningham's second semester at the Academy, they visited Taliesin East, where Cunningham met Wright's wife, Olgivanna (Wright had died in 1959). The student spent the weekend walking the property, absorbing Wright's built disquisition on organic architecture. He especially remembers the haunting quality of a great iron Buddha sitting on a stone pedestal near the main house.

De Czarnecka Lilien asked Cunningham, still a reticent young man with little self-confidence, whether or not he wanted to attend Taliesin, and then suggested he do so, and on her recommendation, he was accepted. In the fall of 1977 he found himself at Taliesin, where he worked as an apprentice for nine months. Cunningham, who brought no talents to the Fellowship such as an ability to play an instrument, felt out of place in the highly ritualized routine and he chafed at the hierarchies that kept him working on what he considered insignificant projects. He felt increasingly that he had to leave what his mentors had hoped would be a haven for his talent.

Today, Cunningham disclaims being a Wright acolyte: For that matter, he resists practicing under the authority

Above left: *The Coonley House (1911, Frank Lloyd Wright, architect), in Riverside, Illinois, a community planned by Olmstead and Olmstead, is one of Wright's most influential residences in America.* Right: *Apprentice's tents at Taliesen West in Scottsdale, Arizona; photograph taken in 1976, when Cunningham lived in the tent on the left.*

of any "ism." But one of the major lessons Cunningham absorbed consciously and unconsciously at Taliesin was Wright's theory of organic architecture—that is, growing buildings from the land as intensifications of the landscape. It was a lesson spread by Taliesin and popularized by Wright's writings and charismatic cultural presence, but the logic would find especially fertile ground in the western landscape that Cunningham discovered in the expansive inland valleys of Southern California. The premise of western spatiality was different from that in the more urban East. Context in the West, especially in the far West and Southwest, did not mean the city, but landscape. Space, with an emphasis on the out-of-doors, was an expansive, open, and permeating ethos, not urban, defined, and tight. The Martin House was located on gridded streets in Buffalo's suburbs. The streets of Rancho Santa Fe curve with the rolling contours of the landscape. The boy from industrial Buffalo found himself confronted by a spatial grandeur that must have been as revelatory as landscape as the Martin House was as building.

From the middle and late nineteenth century, after a century of independence, America searched in its arts for national characteristics to distinguish it from Europe, and major themes have distinguished American artists and architects from their European counterparts. Muralists like Albert Bierstadt, who followed Lewis and Clark out West,

brought back the first visual evidence of the grandeur of America in the tableaux they painted—open, expansive, and majestic spaces revealed by clear light under vast skies—and the pervasive influence of this elemental landscape has distinguished the western strain of American architecture from its antecedents in the Old World and on the East Coast.

Traditional European architecture is rooted in the city, in a defensive posture, reflecting relatively fixed social hierarchies; American work, particularly a kind of architecture that has developed in the West beyond the orbit of Europeanized cities of the East Coast, evolves instead out of a sense of boundless and bountiful land, the individual who owns and occupies it, and the democracy that is a fusion of the two. In this tradition, any enterprising spirit—not just well-schooled gentlemen—can design and build: They are Whitman's architectural heirs, and their designs reach out to the land that is at once protector, instructor, and inspiration. The context of nature and the landscape has often prevailed over the context of the city in the practice of Western architects.

After the Philadelphia Centennial exhibition in 1876, Wright and other architects participated in a common search for an indigenous American architecture, famously developing the Prairie School, named after the characteristic landscape of the American heartland. They developed the notion of the house and landscape involved in a reciprocal relationship, with wings stretching into yards, blurring the distinction between inside and out. But that search and the broader implications were equally valid in American landscapes farther west—in the deserts of the Southwest, as Wright himself so brilliantly demonstrated at Taliesin West, but also in the mountain and coastal states. Western landscapes often invited the response of openness rather than the defense of closure—as in the harsher climes of the East Coast. Space in the West tends to separate buildings; Eastern space tends to bring them together in tighter communities.

Just before he decided to leave Taliesin, the Snows invited him to San Diego where Frances Snow Moran's daughter and son-in-law had bought a hilly property in Rancho Santa Fe, outside San Diego. Moran's daughter was thinking of copying her mother's Frank Lloyd Wright house, but her mother dissuaded her, asking Cunningham to look at the property. The couple asked him what he would propose. The question started his practice.

Left: A misty scene in Cazenovia Park, in Buffalo, shows a limited view characteristic of the scenery where Cunningham grew up. Right: The beams and pool of Harmony frame a Southern California landscape that typifies the scenery where he has worked as an architect.

BUILDINGS

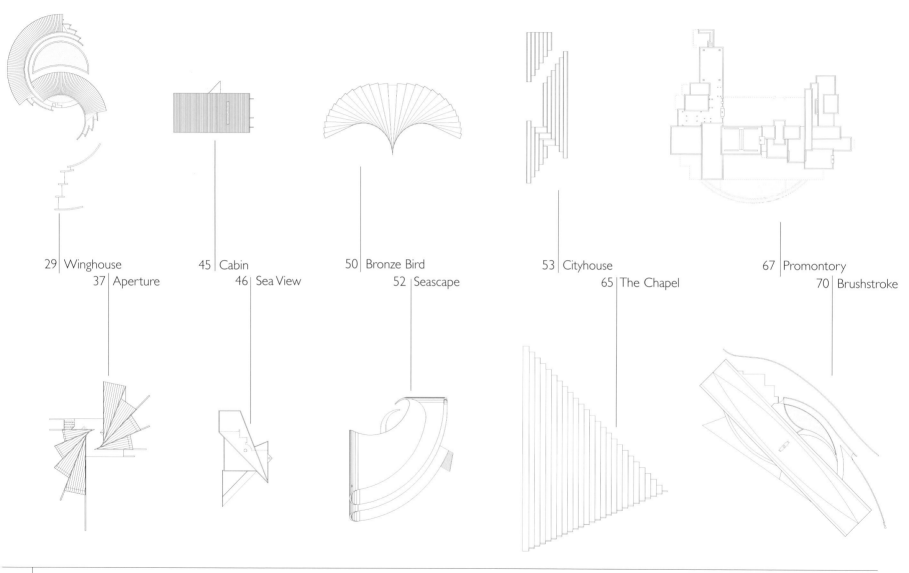

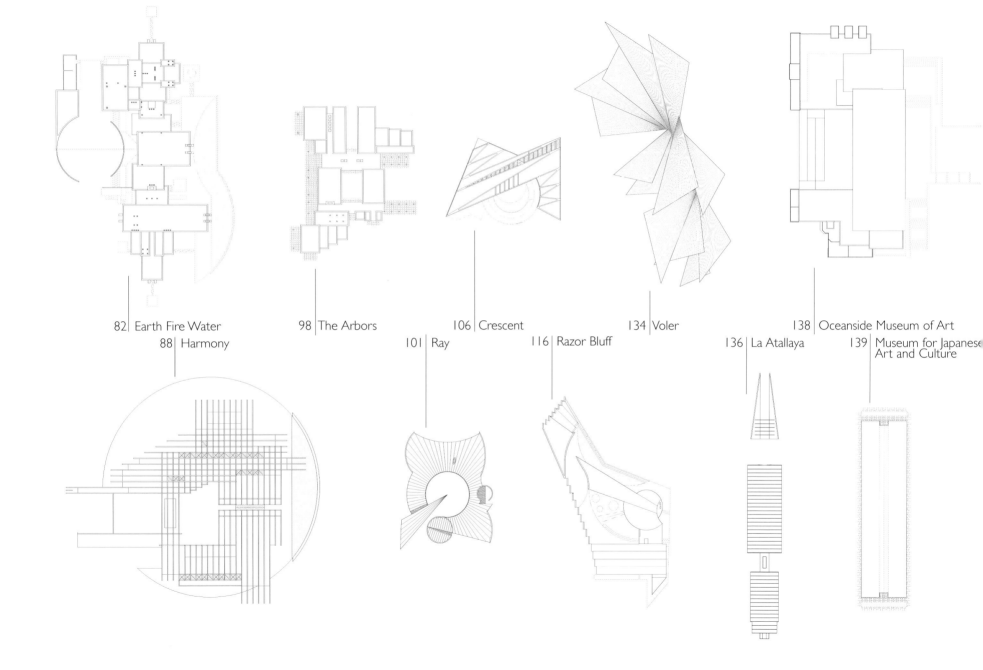

WING HOUSE   In Rancho Santa Fe, twenty-four-year old Cunningham walked and assessed the 4.5-acre site, situated at the confluence of two canyon ravines that flow into a natural bowl. With a branch, Cunningham drew in the dirt an idea for a plan, sketching a pair of semicircles spiraling out in opposite directions from a central point.

The curves, like two opposing swings of a compass, traced the geometry of the canyons, following the shape of the knoll along its topographic lines. Cunningham avoided the practical convention of siting the building on the flat part of the site. His concept for the house, which grew out of the landscape, channeled what he sensed were its forces. Responding to the hillside it helped shape, the S-shaped plan reached to the back and front yards, the arcs cupping space inside and outside in continuous flows. The curvilinear movement of the land encouraged curvilinear movement in the house: Cunningham was using curves to express motion. The designer broke the box, eschewing contained, static space in favor of open geometry and form.

The underlying theme of Wing House is rotation. The center is a void—implied but not visible—but the center holds the composition. Cunningham designed the house around the idea of two stones thrown into a pool, creating ripples. Left: The roof and pool area. Right: The back garden.

The scheme was literate, resonating in principle with some of Wright's circular projects. But Cunningham's plan was more gestural and less geometrically controlled, and the design eschewed any notion of craft in favor of an abstraction whose disappearing details emphasized line and shape over joinery and the display of materials. Unlike Wright's curvilinear designs, with circles embedded in grids that provided an underlying measure and sense of control, Cunningham's spinning design released the house into the landscape in a movement that was simultaneously centripetal and centrifugal. Cunningham was not the first architect to pinwheel a plan—R. M. Schindler configured his own house on North Kings Road in West Hollywood in 1922 with squared wings that embraced the yard—but Cunningham unleashed his house into the landscape with a remarkable degree of freedom that was still tethered conceptually to a control point, like a riff still tied to a set musical structure. The gesture was based in a geometrically rigorous concept.

Cunningham, who himself did not take to highly structured academic situations, followed cultural pursuits on his own, and he explains the play not in Wrightian terms but as a function of jazz and jazz notation. "The tapping on instruments, using the back side of the bow, the sliding of notes" prompted him to seek in

this design moments of counterpoint, the void to the solid, the float to the fixity. Cunningham came to Rancho Santa Fe with a developing sensibility and perhaps a nascent approach to design, but his architectural philosophy was hardly set, and he looked outside the field to find a design rationale: "You can make architecture out of anything: a broken teacup, a piece of music, a woven basket."

Designed from 1978 and finished in 1982, at about the time Frank Gehry completed his own house in Santa Monica, Wing House represented an original reinterpretation of Wright and even Lautner, then working in a richly expressive curviplanar idiom materialized in concrete. The East Coast press, which never published Wing House despite the attention it received in local publications, had stereotyped Modernism as a dry style without complexity and contradiction, and hardly took notice of far more established figures like Lautner. Wing House was an inspired design carried off with a maturity remarkable for an architect in his mid twenties building his first work.

Cunningham developed the initial idea through working drawings, which he then shepherded through various stages of official approval. But the house as conceived was not possible at the time because of local design review board requirements, and because of

technological limitations. Cunningham had specified a copper roof that would fan out with the curving forms of the two wings, but the review board required instead either a Spanish tile roof or wood shakes, and Cunningham opted for the lesser of the two evils— wood. Still, the shakes contradicted the aesthetic of a roof that, in spinning, wanted to taper to a thin, cutting edge. Elsewhere, thick wood mullions stopped the eye, arresting the movement, especially in the living room skylight. The board also required that Cunningham change the poured-in-place concrete walls to concrete block covered in stucco. The surface treatment domesticated the wall, robbing the shapes of their material power. Under pressure from the committee, the voids that Cunningham intended to fill with sleek planes of glass ceded to heavy wood mullions that interrupted the flow of the lines defined by the edge of the roof. Wood in the eyes of the review board imported a desirable measure of rusticity to the suspiciously abstract design.

Fortunately, some twenty years later when new owners bought the house, Cunningham was able to revisit the project. A new design review board allowed the copper roof and butt-jointed glazing technology, which permitted continuous walls of curved glass. This time around, Cunningham had a budget sufficient for limestone floors inside that would continue, without a level

ROOF PLAN

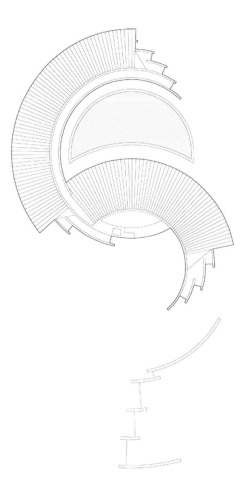

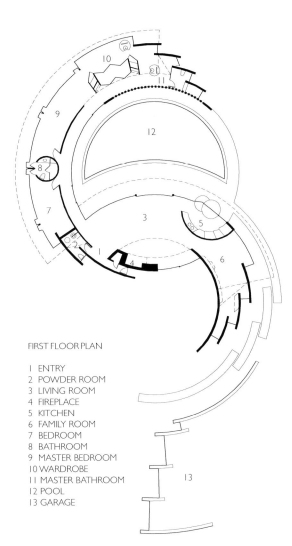

FIRST FLOOR PLAN

1 ENTRY
2 POWDER ROOM
3 LIVING ROOM
4 FIREPLACE
5 KITCHEN
6 FAMILY ROOM
7 BEDROOM
8 BATHROOM
9 MASTER BEDROOM
10 WARDROBE
11 MASTER BATHROOM
12 POOL
13 GARAGE

change, past the glass enclosure to limestone paving outside: The floor plane was continuous. After nearly a quarter century at the boards, Cunningham had mastered the art of detailing so that he was fully capable of achieving in the field the construction finesse that the concept wanted.

Cunningham at last was able to eliminate extraneous elements and simplify the lines, to return to his core idea of roofs floating over radiating walls. He reduced the elements to just the structure of the house and the glass voids, embellished only by cherry cabinetry, which he chose to echo the coloration of the bark of the manzanita bushes on the property. The visible material palette consisted only of cherry, limestone, glass, copper, and smooth-troweled plaster. Just as Lautner, his friend, colleague, and companion Taliesin fellow in Los Angeles, improved on his original designs when technology caught up to the vision, Cunningham was able to bring the house up to its original concept.

With Wing House, Cunningham established not only his practice in San Diego, but also a direction and themes that he would pursue and develop. Clearly, when he arrived in San Diego, he imported instincts developed over years of being exposed to Wright: He listened to the site and specifically to the fall of the land and built in response to its contours in what emerged as a synergistic relationship. The site itself, backed up to the hills,

isolated the house from others in the neighborhood, so nature itself—the vegetation, sun exposure, view orientation, ruggedness, magnitude—constituted the context to which he responded. This was not the place or moment for meekness: The house was just 3,800 square feet, and therefore not large by the standards of this affluent community, but Cunningham was making no small conceptual plans. The house exhibited a precocious professional self-confidence.

What Cunningham exhibited in his first project was a predilection for complexity, which inhered in the geometry of two circles spinning out in opposite directions from their common overlap. At the Wing House, Cunningham started to cultivate an architecture that could not be understood at first glance, but required a promenade that would yield an understanding. The spinning arms propel occupants into the hilly yard: The exploration through the house and into the site delivers all the physical advantages of California's out-of-doors, for which Cunningham had broken the circle and opened form.

Cunningham did not build motion into the geometry

Water features that surround the house turn it into an object floating in space, as though released from earth and gravity. Reflection in the pool is integral to the visual concept of the house.

simply for the sake of motion—form for form's sake—but to physicalize the house, to make it experiential. The house spins the senses of anyone inside toward the rugged hillscape through banks of windows sheltered under the fanning roof. The house may be beautiful, but it also engages the senses and triggers an emotional response. From the outset, Cunningham's architecture does not fall in the tradition of Modernist objectivity deriving ultimately from the logic of the assembly line and the scientistic ethos of the twentieth century. The house belongs to at least two alternative traditions—the house derives meaning from the landscape, and the narrative of man's integration with the landscape via architecture and dwelling. The forms here supercede mute objectivity through the cultivation of the subjective responses of the occupant. Object and subject are not distinct, but related and interactive: Each occupies and cultivates the space of the other.

Cunningham went to school on the Wing House, learning how to carry the concept for a building through to the working drawings, and how to drive a project through the permit and construction process. The young

The skylight in the living room and the glass wall in the kitchen—expanses of glass without mullions—dissolve the barrier between house and landscape and invite nature into the interiors.

man who had realized at the Martin House that architecture represented a practical, real-world application of art not only built his practice on houses but constructed his own understanding of architecture through the pragmatics of building. Each building has emerged as a tutorial that afforded Cunningham an immersive learning experience. As a case study, each has represented a design solution that has become a building block in his development. He effectively became an architect by the Dewey method: The sometime student basically enrolled in each house by making it, acting then as his own tutor and critic.

A pragmatist by choice and necessity, the self-trained architect augmented his observations from the field with observations drawn from the arts.

Art as a source and inspiration structures his idea of practice, and artistic success for him measures a project's value. His vocation as an artist architect takes priority over his status as a professional. Architecture for Cunningham is not an art, but art.

An accordian-shaped wall of glass in the hallway at left and a curved exterior wall at right accept different types of light at different times of day, creating a sundial effect throughout the house. "People think of architecture as solid," says Cunningham, "but the ephemeral is just as important."

Cunningham has produced, on average, one major house a year, each significantly different from the other. Although his attitude about the importance of the site is consistent, his response to each site varies widely. Without an articulated philosophy, Cunningham brings few assumptions to a project and does not repeat himself.

APERTURE   Cunningham's second house, which he started in 1982, was located on a spectacular promontory in Cardiff-by-the-Sea overlooking the expansive San Elijo Lagoon, at the edge of the Pacific. Working simultaneously from the inside and the outside, he generated the design in a dialogue with the site as he studied and understood it both up close and at a distance.

The view potential was reciprocal: The site commanded a sweeping panorama, which in turn focused on the property, sited at the leading edge of a prominent escarpment. It could be seen from almost every angle, in rotational profile from a nearby freeway, and from restaurants on the south side of the lagoon. Applying his understanding of architecture's potential as art, Cunningham realized that the responsibility of the design was that it consummate the hillside as a piece of public sculpture. The house therefore had a unique potential for contributing to the shared public sphere at a sensitive moment in the visual ecology of the coast.

Cunningham then, did not import a position, or even a formal predilection to the project, but assumed a more understanding posture, asking the site in effect what it wanted the building to be. Sensing the land as though it were a force field, Cunningham felt it move. "It seemed to be rotating in one direction, only to reverse the direction of rotation in the back, and then there was the sweep of the views," he says, implying an additional rotational force. Cunningham conceived a design that would rotate with the forces, which implied two forms turning in opposite directions—not unlike the plan of opposing curves in the Wing House. But since he had just designed that building as a composite of partial circles, he enlisted straight lines to create segments that would give the illusion of rotating movement. The segments themselves

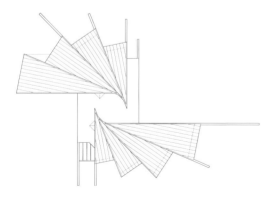

were positioned on the site to capture desired views, forming wedges that turned with the curving contours of the site. On one side, the bluff marries the site where the slope of the hillside elides with the slope of the roof. Cunningham conceived circulation within the house as though rising through chambers of a nautilus, and the ascending progression of terraced rooms, from the lowest bedroom to the highest, culminates

The angles of the bluff face match those of the roof, which raises the earth and spins it into the sky. Aperture's straight lines culminate in a vortex that forces people to look up.

led there by students, once refused to enter), but like much of Goff's work, the house's individuality is induplicably eccentric.

Instead, the individuating characteristic of Cunningham's design within this tradition is its graceful lyricism, while the originality lies in the fact that Cunningham built two spirals turning in opposite directions, split by an entry court. The front door opens into the west spiral, where stairs step down into the living room, with its fanning views of the Pacific to the west. At the back of the space, the room leads under the entry court to stairs in the east spiral, which rise on a path leading to spiraling, wedge-shaped chambers, with adjacent patios, which frame views of the panorama. A loftlike master bedroom at the top of the higher spiral consummates that progression, and its view windows overlook the lower spiral, capturing

Aperture was designed to feature a specific view that is revealed when descending the staircase. The roofs meet only at the apex. Cunningham's design, which uses straight lines to create the illusion of motion, rotates with the forces of nature, implying two forms turning in opposite directions. The spiral shape that is created is an ancient architectural form, but Cunningham's building using two opposing spirals is a new interpretation.

dramatically in pinnacles. At night the house looks like a lantern.

The spiral is, of course, an ancient architectural form with a long tradition, from mosques in the Middle East to Tatlin's Tower in Revolutionary Russia. In the outer orbits of the Wright universe, Bruce Goff in 1950 built the Babinger house that spiraled around a mast in Oklahoma (a house that Mies van der Rohe,

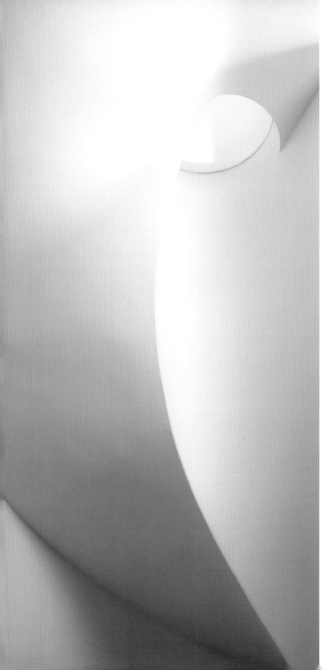

sunset vistas. Cunningham split the form but reconciles the separation inside with a path that sutures together the house s two halves.

With Aperture, as he calls it, geometry emerged even more importantly than it did in the Wing House as a design generator. Each wedge is a triangle, and he deploys the wedge in both plan and section adjusting each for size, height, and view as the basic building block of the structure. With interior terraces, Cunningham solves the classic California problem of circumnavigating challenging hillside slopes by inventing a building section at least as ingenious as any by R. M. Schindler. The famous Austrian architect (and former Wright apprentice) specialized in Los Angeles hillside houses (he also built the influential El Pueblo Ribera courtyard housing in La Jolla of 1923). The eleven levels in Cunningham s 3,500-square-foot Aperture operate as a stepladder up and down the site. Like a fun house, it is disorienting and reorienting.

Because the view and the desirable sun exposure did not necessarily coincide, Cunningham split the roof form, using each step in the wedge to create clerestory windows that bring daylight deep into the structure, toward the points of origin of the wedges (farthest from the windows). The outward thrust of each wedge delivers the occupants to the experience of the site

the moon rising, the sun setting, the great color washes at dusk, the careering peregrine falcons. Cunningham instinctively intended to create a form that complemented the hillside, forming an aesthetic beacon within the valley. But the precise form itself that Cunningham eventually devised was the result of a process of discovery rather than a conscious application of a design manifesto. It just seemed to be there, says Cunningham, indicating that the form emerged out of the logic and spirit of the site.

There are numerous forms of Modernism, and Cunningham here in Aperture, despite its nominal connotation, has created an organic structure that builds from the landscape as it immerses the residents in the panorama and its natural phenomena. Counterintuitively, the architect generates circles from straight lines: Carefully calibrated shifts produce the glissando of forms that read so gracefully from afar. Cunningham, who may have a well developed architecture library, has never read architecture periodicals regularly, and he consciously resists trends. But the direction he intuitively pursued with Aperture coincided with a larger critique of the Modernism that emphasizes structure and function. The forms of the house, without easily visible support, seem suspended, and the lightness releases the roof shape to its own antigravitational spin, accelerating its sense of motion and ascent. The building emerges as a visually poetic form, a pas de deux, that indeed has become a local landmark. Cunningham already understood, by training and temperament, the necessity of reverence for a site. What he learned at Cardiff was a lesson about sheer architectural presence: "This was the house where I realized that there was an incredible power in shape," he says.

American architects who are not trained within an academy identified with a doctrine often respond instead to what they consider a higher calling, nature. Southern California, a victim of rampant suburbanization, still has many unbuilt or lightly built areas that resist sprawl. In the early 1980s, Cunningham was practicing in an area of San Diego with an ethos resolutely rooted in land conservation, not only in the highly protected coastal zone but also inland. The modus operandi that evolved as Cunningham designed was to look to the site as a piece of nature—its contours, the views, the exposures—from which to abstract ideas.

Top right: This photo shows a triangle, the basic constituent element of Aperture. Right and left: At Aperture, light seems to rush across the landscape and, after entering the house, climbs the building, sculpts the interior and imports notions of time, season, and the elements into the building.

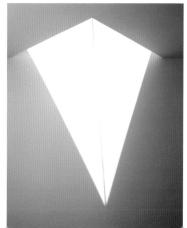

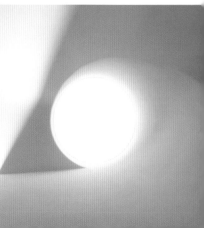

Since Rousseau, and even much earlier in Western tradition, nature has meant many things to many artists. Cunningham believes that there is "an innate power in the ground" and that architects should design structures that compound the power. "The problem for architects is how to increase that power with their buildings." Cunningham is often compared to Wright because of the Taliesin connection, and though he admires Wright at Fallingwater, for example—for setting up the house to take advantage of what he calls "the natural forces of the earth"—Cunningham invents his own interpretation. Through his self-formation as an architect, Cunningham certainly developed affinities to other architects, but if he could be called a spiritual descendent of Wright, he is a collateral relative not in the direct patrilineal genealogy. Cunningham, fiercely independent, has not bonded to any movement or school, and his curiosity led him to

This small house is nestled in the pines at the top of a mountain range. The living spaces on the second level of the house elevate occupants so that they are level with the tree line, and feel as though they are living among its branches. At night, away from the city, the windows frame an unpolluted, almost mythic night sky. Cunningham uses the roof to edit the elements and shape the experience of being in nature.

seek inspiration not only outside Taliesin but also outside the field altogether.

For both the Wing House and Aperture, Cunningham responded to the contoured sites with curvilinear geometries that gave the impression of being more gestural rather than controlled: As spinning and spiraling forms, they generated energy. Cunningham was not only at home in the curvilinear world, but prone to relaxing the controlling geometries, edging them toward greater freedoms. The forms are more lyrical than Euclidean. "People use the ninety-degree angle as a terrible crutch," says Cunningham. "I think the right angle was pushed to standardize things. It's fairly unnatural."

CABIN   Few houses are more formally and spiritually empathic with nature than the small cabin Cunningham designed for Horton and Diana Sherwood in 1985 in Julian, a mountain resort near San Diego, with gently contoured, densely forested hills. "I felt the house should have a close relationship with the ground," he says. The copper-washed roof begins just above ground level, and, supported by two laminated wood beams resting on four columns, the roof seems to sweep the land up over the house in a line arching to the sky. The trajectory stops over the living room on the upper story (this is the first house in which Cunningham reversed floors, situating

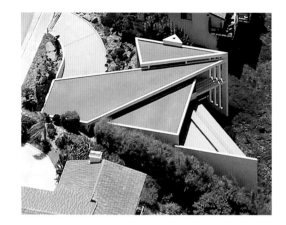

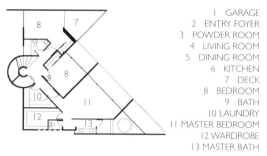

SECOND FLOOR PLAN   FIRST FLOOR PLAN

1 GARAGE
2 ENTRY FOYER
3 POWDER ROOM
4 LIVING ROOM
5 DINING ROOM
6 KITCHEN
7 DECK
8 BEDROOM
9 BATH
10 LAUNDRY
11 MASTER BEDROOM
12 WARDROBE
13 MASTER BATH

the living room on the upper level to capture views and sight lines). Set amid pines on sloping terrain, the house feels like a tree house, an effect intended by the architect. Cunningham uses the roof to cultivate the seasons. Wright designed for snow, creating ledges within stone walls that received snow like line etchings. Cunningham here conceived the roof to catch and sculpt snow: In winter it lingers on the arching roof like a billowing white blanket. The copper itself will acquire a patina over time.

Just as the roof curves in section, the walls below curve in plan. As in Wing House, Cunningham has set two curves playing off each other, but this time simultaneously in the x, y, and z dimensions. The architect elegantly reconciles the curves topologically by lifting the roof off the walls, creating clerestory windows that wash light across the arching ceiling. By removing the windows from the walls and avoiding visually disruptive punctures, Cunningham maintains the flowing lines of curved walls playing off curves. The volumetric design recalls the sculptural plasticity of John Lautner's houses, but rendered here in redwood rather than concrete: The house seeks agreement with the wooded context and does not stand out in heroic apposition. Still the house, a succinct but robust presence, makes no apologies.

Cunningham's achievement here is to orchestrate in three dimensions, not just in plan, the sense of movement he has started cultivating in the earlier projects. There is a graceful inevitability to a complex design that in no way seems forced.

SEA VIEW   When he starts a design, Cunningham visits the site at different times of day to understand how it behaves at different hours. Although he speaks of the land, he means the larger environment as experienced from the land. "Everything is designed from the land's point of view, the views that are presented to it, the light as it appears," he says. "What the views will be and how the light will come is almost all you need to know for a building. It's almost like having a camera and planning a shot.

Sea View is on a steep, challenging, landlocked site. Cunningham focused the view on the ocean, specifically on a particular surfing spot that the owner loved. The surf can be seen from every room in the house. Above: The roof and interior plans. Right: The ocean facade.

You know what you want to see, and design how you are going to frame it."

Sometimes the houses are so focused on nature that, in featuring the landscape at the exclusion of surrounding buildings, they ignore the neighbors. For Sea View, a house designed for an internationally prominent surfing photographer, Jeff Divine, Cunningham edits out nearby buildings with shuttering walls that channel the views from the dining room, living room, bedroom, and master shower into view corridors focused on a legendary section of the shore called Cottons Point. The house emerges as a lens through which occupants look at the surrounding landscape. Cunningham frames views from the inside, and in their bracketed domain, the occupants enjoy the illusion that they alone possess and occupy the view. The house draws its meaning from the object of its gaze.

By conventional suburban standards, and even by professional standards, Cunningham's first half-dozen

Left: Because of the acute steepness of a sloping site that does not permit standing, this expansive terrace is needed as outdoor living space. Right: Sunset and sunrise are salient moments in Southern California's beach and surf culture, and the huge windows present a show of sun, sand, and waves which the building frames and invites into the building.

houses were unusual in their poetic grace and environmental wisdom. But after nearly a decade of practice, through the mid- to late-1980s, Cunningham's houses still looked like the late-modern houses they were and though much transformed, they usually resonated with established precedents, especially with buildings done by members of the outer rings of Frank Lloyd Wright's circle. But for Cunningham each house was a stepping stone into deeper architectural waters, and he never retreated: The more he dared, the farther he ventured.

BRONZE BIRD   Starting in 1987, Cunningham broke
through the boundaries of his practice and designed
houses with a strong metaphoric content. They looked
like the inspiration they represented more than any
conventional notion of architecture, structure, and
building. Some suffered from literalism, but collectively
they brought his voice into new poetic territory.
Metaphor visualized through an abstract minimalist aes-

thetic removed him from a strictly architectural genealogy, and a dependency on geometry.

An intuitive designer, he often seizes on a catalyst
triggered by a particular facet of the program, including
the personalities and backgrounds of the clients. For a
house on a lakeside in the Cuyamaca Mountains near
San Diego, Cunningham devised a bird with the reduc-
tive simplicity of a Brancusi. Cunningham took his cues

from the rotations of a natural bowl at the site created
by an ancient landslide; with swirling forms, he transformed the idea into the figure. Louis Sullivan and
Wright took images from nature and cast them in buildings, but Cunningham interprets nature visually through
the abstracting lens of a more Modernist practice.

Cunningham seldom remains representational but
he distills an initial idea or form to achieve a shape

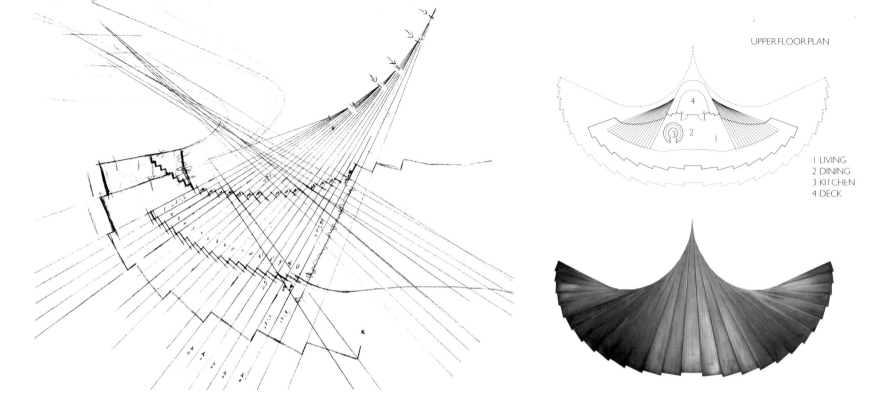

1 LIVING
2 DINING
3 KITCHEN
4 DECK

simplified to a clear figure. In this case, he hybridized the emerging rotational shape of the bowl with an image taken from a Chinese calligraphic scroll once owned by the mother of the client, Chandler Ward. The text relayed a story of wild geese flying over the reflection of a moon in a lake: The image symbolized success and prosperity. The client's hillside property faced a pond and forested hillside on one side and a long view to Lake Cuyamaca. To evoke the image of wild geese leaving one lake for another, Cunningham cast the house as a bird taking wing, just the tips of the feathers touching ground. The feathers of the wings formed a wingspread that covered a large open interior space like a cape open to the long view. The legendary engineer T. Y. Lin reviewed the daring structure: It was buildable.

The client expressed few demands in his brief for a one-bedroom house. He did, however, have a rarefied sensibility, which became the basis of the program. Inventing a

Bronze Bird is based on the rotation of a simple triangle. Each triangle drops slightly to create the downward motion of the feathers. The roof is covered in bronze, and a pearlescent plaster surfaces the base.

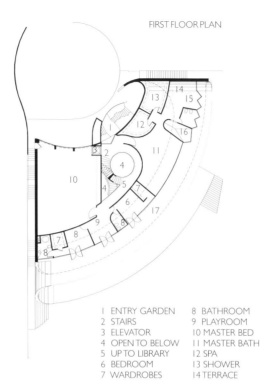

1 ENTRY GARDEN	8 BATHROOM
2 STAIRS	9 PLAYROOM
3 ELEVATOR	10 MASTER BED
4 OPEN TO BELOW	11 MASTER BATH
5 UP TO LIBRARY	12 SPA
6 BEDROOM	13 SHOWER
7 WARDROBES	14 TERRACE

house with a qualitative rather than quantitative program is a rare and difficult task that forces architects to commit to forms that represent the essence of their architecture. This project without a program revealed Cunningham's underlying desire to create purely sculptural objects, and the literal visualization of flight revealed a characteristic latent in his earlier work—that (unlike Wright, who anchored his houses with massive fireplaces) Cunningham

preferred to detach the building from its gravitational obligations. Wing House spins, and Aperture rises as it spins. Cunningham was not interested in the landscape only in its earthbound sense but in its broader panorama, which included notions of sky, air, and water.

The significant shift in the design approach represented by Bronze Bird was the building's pronounced figural content. In a century whose dominant strain of modernist

architecture was predicated on the objective standards of mass production and scientific methodology, Cunningham was reaching to an obscure and exotic text to structure the imagery of the building. He was abandoning the century's well established, subconsciously cherished notions of objectivity to cultivate poetic subjectivity. Eero Saarinen had of course used the image of a flying bird at his TWA building at JFK Airport, and Cunningham's Bronze Bird was only confirming his own already established proclivity to design buildings with a high degree of expressiveness. But the visual metaphor of the bird drove Cunningham's design trajectory even farther into purely emotive territory. The word led the way, and it was liberative. Cunningham's own arguments— "I don't build houses. I build pieces of art, and people live in them"—exhibited an intellectual abruptness that fell short of the gathering complexity of designs whose richness was now explicitly compounded by poetic content.

The house was not built, nor were any of the other four projects done for the same client. All architects contend with the mortality rate of projects, but the more adventuresome projects at least qualify as paid office research and often serve as catalysts for progressive evolution.

SEASCAPE   In 1990, Cunningham produced Seascape, and here he harnessed the power of metaphor to drive the most convincing, and complex, of the series. As in Bronze Bird, the final design derived from the hybridization of two images. Visiting the site, looking for visually poetic cues that distinguished the property, Cunningham saw a huge pine tree whose branches had been twisted by the ocean winds. He morphed this image with the image of the waves cresting at the bottom of the promontory to create a house that swirled in both plan and section. Cunningham was not literally representing either the branches or the waves, but evoking the swaying and cresting forms by building continuous motion into the house. Curving floor planes turned up to become curving walls that turned back again in other curving floor planes: Cunningham was proposing the house as an occupied Möbius strip. In his earliest projects, he understood the power and movement of the land, but after a decade Cunningham was looking at nature in its widest terms, capturing the sea and vegetation not as picture images but as phenomena living in time.

At Seascape, the entire project is based on the preference to preserve the natural contours of the site and to minimize grading. The implied movement in the structure is inspired by the movement of the waves and the branches of pine trees. Above right: A photomontage of a model of the house on a picture of the site.

Avoiding intellectual analysis, Cunningham resorts to his position of architecture practiced as art to explain the underpinnings of his vision: "Like Cezanne, I take objects and fundamentals as I know them and abstract them into art. I take people's lifestyles, views, and light and turn them into art constructions."

CITYHOUSE   After his highly experimental series of metaphoric designs, the next major commission presented an unusual challenge, as the site, located in the village of La Jolla on an urban block, had virtually no topographic features or view and little direct sun exposure. He was deprived of the talismanic cues that usually jump-start his

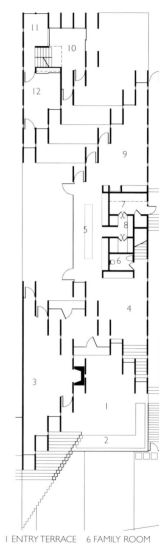

1 ENTRY TERRACE   6 FAMILY ROOM
2 POND   7 LAUNDRY
3 LIVING ROOM   8 PANTRY
4 DINING ROOM   9 POWDER ROOM
5 KITCHEN

SECOND FLOOR PLAN

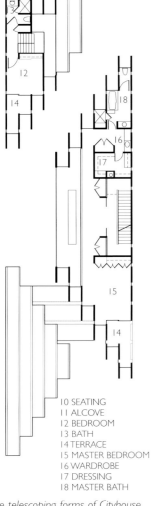

10 SEATING
11 ALCOVE
12 BEDROOM
13 BATH
14 TERRACE
15 MASTER BEDROOM
16 WARDROBE
17 DRESSING
18 MASTER BATH

The telescoping forms of Cityhouse,

as seen from the street

imagination. There was nothing "natural" to which to respond, just the limitations of a long, narrow site bounded on two sides by tall, uninspired, shadow-casting houses. The only significant feature to the otherwise flat parcel was a ten-foot drop at the street. Frank Lloyd Wright never quite felt comfortable designing in urban contexts, and this kind of site prevented the "organic" response that might be expected of a former Taliesin student.

Cunningham, however, did not and does not confine himself to the Taliesin identity, and without a recognizable calling card announcing his position, he explained himself to his potential La Jolla clients, Judith and Bennett Greenwald, by adapting his phrase about living in art: "I do one-of-a-kind sculptures for people to live in." In the early 1980s, only Frank Gehry noted that art had directly influenced his work, but even Gehry backed away from calling his work art. It was a radical position.

Left: *Elements of the façade seem interwoven when seen from some angles.* Right: *From other angles, the elements are seen as independent structures. The concrete forms of Cityhouse interact with the infinite sky; at some times, they read as positive figures against the sky, and at others, the negative patterns of shadow and void between the forms become salient.*

Judging by the extensive thirty-page program the clients drafted in advance of their meeting, Cunningham expected a large property rather than a narrow slot of land. But the 50-by-160-foot lot on La Jolla's main street hardly allowed sufficient visual exposure to support a sculptural response. From Chicago, the clients imported their preference for a pedestrian lifestyle to Southern California, and they chose a site that would allow them to walk everywhere in this cultivated town—restaurants, the Athenaeum, the contemporary art museum. Yet the program called for a house in California, a spacious and luminous environment in a garden setting.

If the house would not enjoy breathing room, Cunningham had to create a sense of generosity within the house itself. The internalized typology of a townhouse that would naturally fit the site, however, would not cultivate the sun, light, and spaciousness that the Greenwalds anticipated in their adopted beach community. Stressing the demands on the limited site was the clients' requirement for creating a gallery-like environment for the couple's extensive collection of contemporary art.

The narrow site, minus the side yard setback requirements, prejudiced the design toward orthogonality. Cunningham here could not depend on the site as a positive cue for a responsive design, but had to

instead invent the physical rationale for a self-contained world. Without dependency on a site, he was forced to invent ideas and themes, and his solutions would prove foundational for his further development.

Greenwald, the son of the developer who had hired Mies van der Rohe to design the Lake Shore Towers in Chicago, was a developer in his own right. The presence of Mies in his clients' background and psyche prompted Cunningham to acknowledge the master: "I knew there had to be a clarity and unmistakable directness about the building," he recalls. "I wanted a purity."

The primary problem for a site blinkered by tall houses was how to bring daylight into the interior, and how to expand its sense of space. It was in the morning shadow of one building, and the afternoon shadow of another. The southern exposure was the narrowest part of the lot.

The structural fins of Cityhouse frame views into the garden and cityscape beyond, but understanding a house that does not reveal itself at a glance requires exploration. In the living room (far left) windows from stories above allow light to descend and penetrate. View windows are vertical. The building acts as a giant sun baffle. The kitchen (left) opens to the garden. Walls are near each other, but don't touch (right).

Rather than centering the house on a lot, creating front and back facades facing the street and a back garden, Cunningham brought the garden to the center of the house so that the building cupped the garden in an elongated C configuration, with glass walls facing the small landscaped yard. The house would meditate on a Japanese garden that it defined, which itself is centered on a pond. The garden was the object centered on the lot, and its centering effectively dispersed the house to the perimeter of the site. Normally designed as an object, the house became the field, while the field became the object. Decentering the house and breaking its "objecthood" would prove a seminal insight in subsequent designs. Cunningham had admired the way Wright's Martin House took over the land: He was doing the same in La Jolla but field-reversing figure and ground.

The Japanese famously extend space by borrowing views, hinting at infinity, and the Chinese, by subdividing space into ever smaller parts, expanding toward the infinitesimal. Cunningham devised his own formal techniques

The interior garden becomes part of the rooms that surround it, and, through reflection, the house becomes part of the garden as well. Reflected in the garden pond (right) the sky and house lose their anchors.

for enlarging the sense of space. By breaking walls into panels and stepping them in plan so that they cross the site diagonally, Cunningham elongated the building by forcing occupants to walk along a series of hypotenuses that the panels define. Sometimes he doubles the distance, intentionally halving the efficiency: For example, guests enter the house through a front patio deeply indented in the body of the house, only to walk back to the front in the living area. The architect also breaks the body of the house into three pavilions—the front living room; the main body of the house, with the kitchen below and bedrooms above; and a back study and guest room. Each pavilion masks the next, so that the house can never be seen and completely understood from a single vantage point: It is always angling out of sight, so that, as in an English garden, the end can never be glimpsed. The house itself eclipses the corners of the parcel that would normally signal the defining boundaries.

In Cityhouse, light is introduced as a celestial clock and shifts depending on the time of day and year. As the sun changes angles, the light appears as thin as laser beams, then broadens as the day progresses, narrowing again toward evening. Light connects the building to the physical movement of the Earth.

If Wright was the virtuoso of breaking the box in plan so that its wings reach into the landscape they embrace, he was not quite as inventive vertically. Cunningham, unable to reach beyond the postage-stamp boundaries even to borrow a view, reaches up instead, creating vertical slivers of space that rise two and three stories. "I borrowed ceiling spaces," he says. The ceiling, for example, has three heights, and all the spaces overlap vertically or horizontally, borrowing space visually from one another.

The eye, then, is not confined by Wright's low horizon, but reaches diagonally up in the vertical dimension through the porous fabric of segmented walls—just as the body moves on a diagonal. The height of the house is, like the plan, longer by the hypotenuse.

Cunningham may be acknowledging Mies by constructing a house out of simple orthogonal planes. But at the same time, Cunningham subverts the orthogonal, and its primacy, by privileging the invisible diagonal. Cunningham vectorializes the space that in Mies's open-plan buildings is frontal and static. Mies's grids pin space while Cunningham's stepped panels and stepped sections make space slip, giving it spatial dynamic and even thrust.

Unlike many of his colleagues, Cunningham does not elevate these strategies to the level of theory, but develops and understands them empirically. For Cunningham, the hypotenuses in this house are not ideated; they simply constitute longer paths that add apparent size to the house.

Still, the architect is not without ambitions beyond pragmatics. Influenced again by jazz, he tried to make light contrapuntal, cultivating strips of light that act as striations in counterpoint to form. "The way light reacts on shapes, the riffs of light, the rhythms, that's the music of the space," he offers, adding, "The shape has to be pure for the counterpoint to work."

Since Cunningham stacked the building on itself to liberate more than half of the land for a garden, the house necessarily had to be vertical: The verticality of a three-story house potentially blocked sun penetration to the lower floors, so Cunningham configured the building to allow vertical light penetration: While he was borrowing space, he borrowed light. The stepped panels were originally conceived to individuate the single work of art that would hang on each, but cumulatively they act as venetian blinds at the scale of the entire building. Horizontal clerestories cross vertical window slots on an exact module. Light filters through the voids between the panels and through the clerestories, creating bands of light glancing on and off all vertical and horizontal surfaces, revolving kaleidoscopically "so that it's moving and alive," he says. For

Cunningham, the secret to bringing out light as a phenomenon is "to hide the source and force someone to look at a small amount—one sunbeam is much more powerful than the vastness of light in the desert. I like shafts of light that open and close." Light, then, is anything but even, but always changing from broad band to narrow, from intense to what Cunningham calls the "blush"—the gradient of light softly washing a surface.

For first-time visitors who are inevitably led through this house as an unfolding event by their curiosity, the house is an exploratorium of variations on the simple theme of stepped panels acting as baffles. But for Cunningham, light was the ultimate epiphany, and as he frequently does in his buildings, he has returned time and again to photograph the building through all phases of the day and seasons. If each

house yields lessons for an autodidact who seems to remain perpetually open to self-instruction, the most important lesson he culled from Cityhouse is that light is the element that both binds a house, and moves it— the house as sundial. "The houses with light patterns are like living objects, they're kinetic," he says. "The pieces don't move, but the effects of movement are recorded on them."

THE CHAPEL In 1990 Cunningham was commissioned to design a chapel in San Dimas, California. The stepped forms at Cityhouse that were generated by a practical logic may have resulted in shifting patterns of striated light, but striated light itself became the real subject, and object, of the chapel. To make the patterns as strong as possible, Cunningham reduced the design to a remarkably simple pattern-generating structural system. He positioned a score of columns several feet apart, short to tall, and joined the top of each with a beam attached at the far end to its point on a diagonal line drawn on the ground. The space between the columns and beams was glazed with a dark blue glass, so the sun projected light through the interstices, suffusing the space with hazy blue stripes set in unpredictable motion, since the beams all leaned at different angles. Light streamed through the beams and columns east and west, for morning and evening services. The altar was placed in the tallest portion of the structure, and the roof angled down, descending behind parishioners congregated a floor below grade. Worshippers stepped in via a low doorway in a compressed entrance that released them into an expansive space that simultaneously soared and fell.

What Cunningham calls a "chapel of light" had the simplicity of a score by Philip Glass and like those insistently rhythmic scores, slight dimensional variation

in each line produced a subtle work that shifted in effect through small increments of change. The sponsor of the design was a concrete contractor, who failed to convince the congregation to hire him to build the project. Nonetheless, the church would have been stunning in the same way Fay Jones's and Frank Lloyd Wright's chapels acquire a life of their own through light. Cunningham counts Jones's chapel and Wright's Wayfarers' Chapel in Los Angeles, as among the few buildings he knows that also produce the light and shade patterns that supercede form in presence and importance.

Chapel was designed to be constructed with post-tension concrete planks that span a wide congregational space in a stepped profile whose gaps project banded light inside that changes continuously. Above: Chapel's Roof plan.

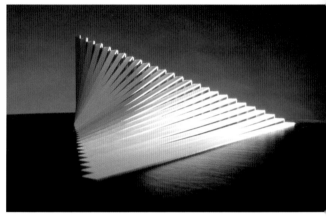

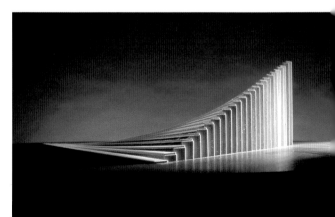

PROMONTORY Interpreting the landscape through architecture, Cunningham was producing houses that were themselves works of art. The designs attracted collectors who, understandably, wanted to add architecture to their collection. Meanwhile, the collections themselves changed the domestic program. With the art, Cunningham had to respond not only to the exterior context but also to an interior world. The demands of showcasing art within the house while showcasing the landscape outside were potentially competitive In Rancho Santa Fe, Cunningham struck a masterful balance in Promontory, built for Stan and Pauline Foster, who owned both a generous parcel of land with a panoramic view and a ranking collection of large-scale contemporary art. Cunningham had to reconcile plate glass views with commanding tableaus. At the same time, the house had to comfortably accommodate large gatherings, often staged for the charities the couple support.

Mrs. Foster wanted no reference to current architectural trends, but asked instead for a clean, timeless, understated design that could survive inevitable shifts in

Promontory is derived from the very simple shapes that were allowed in a community with strict design guidelines. Cunningham's design objective was purity of form.

style. Cunningham satisfied the local design codes by simplifying the prevailing rancho style into abstract cubic shapes whose plain surfaces continued from outside to inside. He composed the house as a series of solids and voids, with broad expanses of sliding glass walls that open the interior to expansive terraces and a walled front court. Large groups of people easily move between inside and outside.

Just as he later thematized South Africa through his palette of materials and elemental symbols in Earth Fire Water, Cunningham created an abstract world inside Promontory, designing a loftlike gallery environment suitable for contemporary pieces intended for plain white walls. Knowing in advance the pieces in the collection, Cunningham designed for the specific works. Frequently, he bracketed walls with columns that formed niches dedicated to artworks that could preside in a space of their own.

But the masterful stroke in the design was Cunningham's handling of light. The public spaces that include the living and dining rooms are deep, and although walls of windows bordered each side, Cunningham evened the natural light throughout the space by bringing clerestory windows and skylights across the roof. He transformed what would otherwise be windows puncturing the roof by masking the sky-

the living spaces to the kitchen and service areas. In addition to creating ceilings that crest and rise, adding a sense of movement, Cunningham pulses the space by moving the walls in and out, to better define niches that harbor the painting and sculpture. The space is not serial and monotonous but individuated: The artworks claim a space of their own within the niches. Cunningham expands the idea of a niche dedicated to art in the powder room, which, with its sacramental font and concentrational intensity, resembles a small chapel. A clerestory washes light along a wall, illuminating a painting. The architect does not use light as a baroque spectacle but as a gentle bath.

The movement of the ceilings and the luminous glow at the edge of the waves dynamize public spaces that might seem institutional and even vacant without the visual activity. The ceilings frame the space in the same way crown moldings once did, but at the same time, they are a light installation in an expanded field. Cunningham, again, edges architecture beyond design into art.

Ceilings at Promontory seem to float. The living room ceiling (right) consists of three billowing shapes that hide sources of natural and artificial light, which blushes all the walls in the house..

lights with undulating ceiling forms that floated below the ceiling line, hiding the windows themselves from most angles while feathering the light, which bounces off white surfaces. "I wanted to distribute natural light throughout the house in a soft way, not with strong, stark, directional light," he says. "Every time a wall breaks, the ceiling breaks and the clerestory windows are introduced. The floating ceilings touch neither the walls nor the ceilings," he says. "Indirect lighting is tucked in all the interstitial spaces, to create the same effect at night."

There are five ceiling levels in the public spaces, and several different rolling or turning shapes. The ceiling modulations are most intense in the gallery space that houses most of the collection, which runs along the front of the house from the private quarters through

Cunningham makes a point of attentively listening to his clients, even to their off-handed remarks, and in response to a casual statement that Mrs. Saltman made about wanting never again to clean gutters, the architect designed a self-cleaning roof: He devised a curved roof shaped like an enormous scupper; the geometry of the inverted curve, which collected rainwater at the center, eliminated gutters. Mrs. Saltman, who has a strong artistic sensibility, also expressed a desire for the house to exhibit a sense of age, but without resorting to historicizing forms. The architect decided to structure the house with old timbers, which he found through a wood broker in Northern California: The massive 800-year-old members were recycled from a dismantled water tank. Cunningham used the timber as posts in a colonnade lining the two sides of a long, linear house set on the elevated plinth. With glazed walls front and back, inset with sliding glass doors, the house is a glass pavilion in the garden, but the ancient timbers and mythopoetic roof shape confer the aura of a Shinto shrine on the structure. Under the curving roof, which bellies inside the house, rooms are organized en suite, and the kitchen and living and dining rooms front terraces on two sides, so that the interiors extend visually outside. A ramp leads up from the entry gate, past a black-bottomed pool shaped like an attenuated leaf. Another ramp leads down to the back garden.

BRUSHSTROKE   In 1995 all of the discoveries that Cunningham had made during his fifteen years of practice converged on a masterful house in La Jolla, designed for Paul Saltman, a biologist, and his wife, Barbara. The Saltmans had lived on the property for thirty years in a one-story ranch house that gradually lost its view across the mesa to the ocean as the surrounding land was developed. An objective of the program was to elevate the house and lift the structure off the ground to return the view (and to avoid the humidity of natural springs on the property). With the yard continuing under an elevated plinth carrying the structure, the house no longer forms a barrier between front and back, and contours of the front and backyards are reconnected as a continuous landscape.

The house displays Cunningham's ability to entirely recast and reorganize a site by sensitively deploying a house within a landscape that the design itself reshapes. Cunningham brings the driveway up to the elevated structure on a ramp, whose retaining walls are gestural: Their calligraphic shapes inspired the house's name, Brushstroke. Cunningham's formal virtuosity is most keenly evident in the extraordinary pool, whose surfaces are flush with the front terraces. Cunningham takes the pool out of the ground, and isolates it from any perimeter walls, and uses the space between the pool and exterior walls as a passage. He brings visitors in from the front gate between the side of the pool, surfaced in black glass mosaic, and the high stuccoed perimeter wall so that they walk past the length of the pool, whose waters brim over the knifelike edges of the infinity rim, to ripple down the black wall.

After the compression within this carefully choreographed sequence of space and materials, guests arrive in the open on the plinth at the front of the house,

Right: *The door to the courtyard was made from recycled wood from an old water tower; scrap pieces were turned into pyramids..* Left: *The wall of the driveway curves in step with the garden wall and the undulating shadow it projects on the stone drive.*

FLOOR PLAN

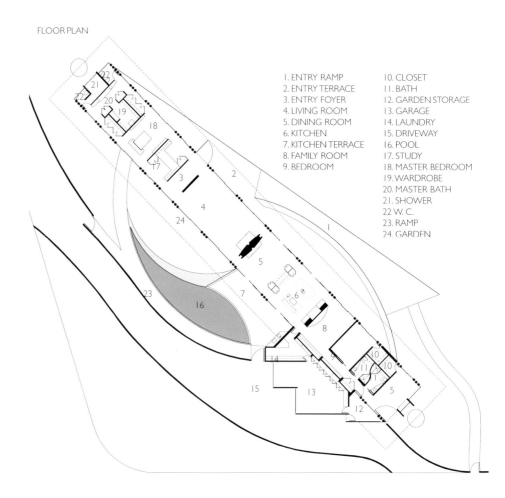

1. ENTRY RAMP
2. ENTRY TERRACE
3. ENTRY FOYER
4. LIVING ROOM
5. DINING ROOM
6. KITCHEN
7. KITCHEN TERRACE
8. FAMILY ROOM
9. BEDROOM
10. CLOSET
11. BATH
12. GARDEN STORAGE
13. GARAGE
14. LAUNDRY
15. DRIVEWAY
16. POOL
17. STUDY
18. MASTER BEDROOM
19. WARDROBE
20. MASTER BATH
21. SHOWER
22. W. C.
23. RAMP
24. GARDEN

The exit driveway and curvature of Brushstroke's

upturned roof seen over the garden wall.

where they face the serene, templelike exterior that the high, opaque walls had baffled from view. Cunningham has controlled the entry sequence so that it becomes a promenade that delivers the surprise of an isolated, very serene world. The "temple" front is mirrored by the black-bottomed pool whose rimless edge creates a pure plane of watery blackness. The sinuous curves of the pool's sides play off one another as they taper to their tip. In the late afternoon, they—and their shadows—also play off the curving front walls. Keeping the pool separate, Cunningham multiplies edges so that the curves of the pool and walls conspire to form a virtual drawing in space in which all the lines evolve and revolve around each other in a relational three-dimensional tableau. The pool is embedded in a visually and spatially complex syntax.

The conspicuous beauty and quiet drama belie the sociability of the house. In their old ranch house, guests would arrive at the gate and head straight for the kitchen in what was an open-door social policy the Saltmans maintained for years. Cunningham organized the new house so that the Saltmans drive up into a garage adjacent to the kitchen, and so that guests, too, drive up to that level, or walk up to the kitchen on the ramp leading from the front gate. Once inside the protective walls, people are essentially inside the perimeter

of the house, within the orbit of the kitchen and its hospitality. The ramp by the pool also leads down to a raked garden that flows beneath the house, which passes overhead like a bridge. The graveled area and the bonsai landscaping give this part of the yard a pronounced Japanese sensibility, a visual leitmotif that emerges early in Cunningham's designs. As in Cityhouse and the Arbors, Cunningham has orchestrated all the elements of the house and yard—terraces, walks, courts, levels, fences, and the house itself—into a *gesamtkunstwerk* that embraces the outside as well as inside. He designs architecture not as an object but as a part of a larger field condition.

If Cunningham's fundamental discovery at Cityhouse was light, the epiphany here is water. Swimming pools are common in Southern California, and they appeared in Cunningham's early houses. Wing House encircled a swimming pool, and Cityhouse wrapped itself around a garden centered on a pond. But at Brushstroke, Cunningham's design elevates the swimming pool to

Right: *Water appears as if free-standing in space. All edges are perfectly mitered to create continuous shapes. With water brimming over the top edge of the pool, side surfaces are always wet and glistening.* Left: *Flames from an outdoor fireplace reflect in the pool.*

the level of environmental art, and the pool with its surrounding terraces and walks rivals the house as the centerpiece of the design.

The presiding presence of the pool is due to the combined effect of several small but important design decisions. First of all, he spatializes the pool by elevating it and keeping it detached, so that visitors walk around its contours. He animates its walls, programming the waterfall to ripple down its mosaic surfaces to a rill running at their base. He details the edges so that they come to a single continuous invisible line that holds the water: Without a visible rim, the water appears to float, magically. Reflections therefore are pure, undisturbed by clumsy edges: He delights in the ability of water—"the first mirror," he says—to alter the physics of the building, making it appear to hover in reflection. Cunningham also positioned the pool close to the house so that sunlight would bounce off the surfaces to play on the underside of the curved roof. The blackness makes the pool appear fathomless as it highlights patterns skittering across the surface. "Just as linguists teach people to speak, architects and artists need to teach people to see," he says. "Until it's presented in a way that you're not used to, until you've made it strange or original or unexpected, people won't notice it. I use water to make you see another way."

Its typological and formal resemblance to a temple is not really the reason for the aura of Brushstroke. There is,

instead, a subtext of ephemeral effects that plays on the building and in the forecourt, heightened by the plain, receptive materiality of ancient wood and abstract surfaces that register nuances of light and shadow. The black pool, its surfaces somehow suspended because there is no visible support, makes the forecourt feel antigravitational: The horizontal ground plane has the same visual weightlessness as the abstract wall planes. In the low setting sun, the woods begin to glow, as shadows sculpt the forms and cast curved patterns on the walls behind.

In Buffalo, Cunningham admired Wright's Martin House for taking control of the site. Here the young architect takes control of the space itself not just in plan but also in three dimensions verging on a fourth spiritual plane. With the high walls, Cunningham has edited out the visual distractions of the neighborhood, establishing a cloistered calm, framing the precinct with a serene backdrop that registers, like a screen, projected plays of fragile ephemera. He cleanses the visual palette and evokes calm as a stage necessary to wonder.

Cunningham had long observed the difference between a building that is worldly and one that is religious,

Gravel appears to be stopped in space by a thin stainless steel edge. Water separates cut stone from gravel and from the edge of the pool.

even if they are both churches, and his admiration for spiritual spaces became a possibility and goal for his own designs as his architectural skills matured and his commissions grew. However, the perception came first and early, starting with the Martin and Coonley houses, and continuing through the travels that would be part of his continuing education. "St. Peters is worldly, but not those tiny chapels by Borromini. You've got to look around in Borromini. With Bernini, you don't turn your head because you understand the space immediately when you enter. Gothic cathedrals are otherworldly: You can't see the sources of light, and the height is aspirational."

The nature of environmental mysticism is difficult to explain and even more difficult to design, but Cunningham describes it, saying, "you're looking for the shadow, for the reflection, for the appearance that will make the physical world meditational. It's something for your soul that's elevating and exhilarating, a serenity and wholeness. I can't tell in advance which of my buildings will have it. You're looking for feelings that are beyond the material facts."

The house is totally transparent from one side to the other, and reflections double the image and transparency. Right: Antique redwood columns and a glass wall separate the terrace from the ramp to the garden.

With the example of the Salk Institute's pristine concrete work just up the coast, Cunningham knew that the effects he sought, and that the very concept of auratic space, depend on execution—the detailing, the quality of materials, the craftsmanship. All of these came together in Brushstroke, which elevated the level of Cunningham's work by a full quantum. Having achieved a spiritual feeling in the design, Cunningham identified the qualities he would strive for in all his other projects— "the phenomena that make the physical world special."

House by house, Cunningham's insights, supported by a growing technical expertise, were cumulative, and by the late 1990s, even though no two ever looked much alike, the houses displayed a consistent emotional depth and complexity. Institutional and cultural commissions still eluded the architect who had earned a reputation designing houses, but a few were large enough to have an institutional scale.

Right: *The ground level on which the original house was built is now the site of a forest of redwood columns that raises the new house to capture the view. A rock from the owners' favorite surf spot is raised on a pedestal as a piece of found sculpture.* Left: *A linear skylight that separates the ceiling from the wall striates the curved surface with light.*

a reference to the basic elements—earth, air, fire, and water. His formal vocabulary in this long, sprawling house remained abstract, but he succeeded through palette and symbols in layering the design with associations that gave the house a memory dimension. Cunningham was expanding his territory of exploration by playing to the mind as well as the senses, creating a noumenal world within his phenomenal environment.

Cunningham is always inventive, often in response to such givens in a context as views. But sometimes, as in this commission, he uses his inventiveness to break his way free of constraints. As in many of his projects in communities with design review restrictions, Cunningham had to contend with design standards that favor traditional styles: He complied by shifting the subject. Through a process of abstraction, he simplified the prevailing "rancho" style, honing it down to the Modernist essentials of solid and void. Walls are plain and off-white, and the roof, flat.

But unlike other generous sites in this countryside of rolling hills, the long, narrow parcel was exceptionally restricted. The last lot to be built on in its neighborhood, it offered only a single view in one direction. Cunningham had to negotiate the house into the view by inventing an approach that would tunnel visitors into mystery.

While Le Corbusier starts his promenade architecturale within the building, Cunningham here starts his

EARTH FIRE WATER   Cunningham's houses differ so greatly from one another not only because of the specific quality of each site but also because of the uniqueness of Cunningham's clients. Always thinking of architecture in terms of art, he conceives of each design as a client portrait. San Diego, whose coastal landscape is less urbanized than Los Angeles, has long attracted people from outside the state and even the country, and the architect has

sometimes attempted to cast the house as environmental biography, in the character of his clients' place of origin. The design speaks to memory.

For a family that moved to San Diego from South Africa, Cunningham created a landscape of recollection. The clients brought to their discussions with Cunningham descriptions of a countryside and culture that the architect consciously evoked through his use of materials and promenade with the approach into the property. "I brought the driveway in on the high side, and drive in through an allee of pepper trees, through a tunnel of lacy green, and arrive at a circular motor court, bounded by high walls," he says. Cunningham, then, invented a ceremony of entry, enchanting the visitor into forgetting the fact the entry was blinded to the landscape and panorama that constitute the raison d'etre of the entire development. "The arrival courtyard, with the walls surrounding it, masks everything about location—you're in a cylinder," he clarifies, adding, "The driveway and motor court are gravel. The sound was important to the owners." Cunningham sustains the suspense he created by hiding the entry to the house. A visitor sees only two gaps in the cylinder, and steps forward into either, in the company of a little rivulet originating on the high side of the circular courtyard. "You come forward and then see a set of stairs that angles over and cascades down into the earth, to a landing that is isolated by two reflection pools on either side of the door."

The water that Cunningham starts above the motor court has trickled down the wall of the court and across its surface in a four-inch canal reminiscent of Louis Kahn's famous channel at the Salk Institute, down the retaining wall, to the entry, where Cunningham mixes the idea of water and earth. He adds Africa into the gathering asso-

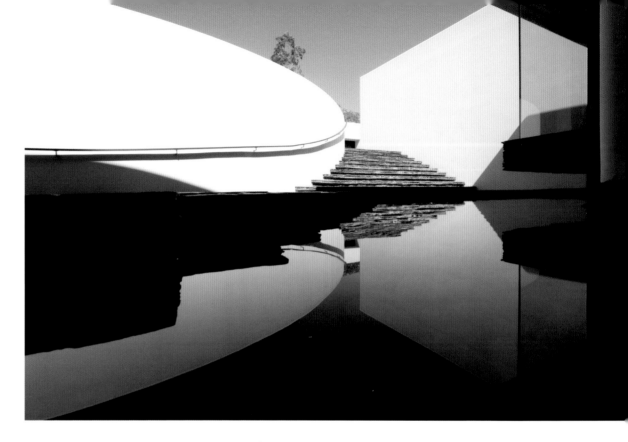

ciations by paving the landing and floors beyond in South African slate, rich in a blend of rust colors, grays, and blacks. Beyond the entry, inside the house, the far side of a long, narrow suite of rooms opens to a wide pool that parallels the back side of the house along its entire width. Two fireplaces, one left and one right of the living room, bracket the space, holding the water in between. "At one

point, you're seeing five bodies of water, or water courses, and the fireplaces," he says. The effect, then, with the fireplaces roaring, is that the house harbors fire and floats

Left and above: *Dual staircases, surfaced in multicolored African slate., are surrounded by pools of water. These photos show them in the front and back of the library.*

like islands in water. You have left the car behind on an upper level, and stepped down into the earth and another more elemental world. Beyond the water, the ground falls away to the view, delivering an aerial feeling: "You have a sense of liftoff into space and air," says Cunningham.

The family collects tribal art, and Cunningham chose a palette that gives the dark, crafted pieces a material and chromatic home. With its oranges and reds embedded within a shadowy background, the slate complements a dark, very grained African wood, afrormosia, that

Above: An aerial view of the pool. Left: The dining room is an island between the entry pool and the swimming pool. Right: The residence reflected in the swimming pool. Sliding walls of glass open the house so that furniture groupings feel as though they are out of doors.

Cunningham has used in built-in closets and furniture. Together, the wood and slate give the tribal pieces a visual ground, conferring the sense that the pieces belong here. For a site whose own grounds are limited, Cunningham has conjured an entire continental landscape, inventing a narrative into a space of culture that he cultivates through materials and symbols. Cunningham deepens the sense of earthiness with a choice of plants that evokes Africa.

Cunningham reinforced his ambitious aesthetic aims with a masterful plan with a perimeter that expands and contracts, inviting the outside in and pushing the inside out, in a sensitive reinterpretation of the garden pavilion. The house is zoned for activity and open to encourage flow, rather than bounded with walls. Wide windows, framed in wood, pivot to the surrounding terraces so that the living room furniture appears to be sitting on a continuous patio when all the doors are open. The center of the house, large enough for entertaining, opens to both sides, so that light is balanced. The spaces feel like an open-air camp. "I was trying to get a sense of savannah, with breezes blowing through and just a roof over your head."

The pool accentuates the length of the long, linear plan: "it elongates everything," he says, "and all the rooms open onto the pool, and the reflections of the water help lift everything up, the light bouncing off the ceilings.

HARMONY At about the time Cunningham was finishing Earth Fire Water he began designing another house for other clients with roots in South Africa—though the geographical biography was broader because of time spent in Switzerland and Japan. Through their travels, they had become connoisseurs of landscape.

Cunningham purposely designed their 10,000-square-foot house, on the crest of a knoll, to capture the sweeping 300-degree panorama, with valleys and hills rolling to the foothills, while focusing the house on the cardinal features of distant mountains.

Practicing as an artist architect rather than as a businessman architect, Cunningham seldom delegates design work, especially in its initial formative stages, and much like R. M. Schindler decades before, who made many decisions on site, Cunningham himself visits the site from the start of the commission: The site is always the point of idea genesis. Cunningham of course retreats to the office to sketch, and early on, the sketches are turned into study models: The highly spatial concepts can best be

Previous pages: *The first impression of Harmony, seen from the entry gate. The house is built around a three-dimensional grid.* Left: *The main gate to the courtyard is a large onyx slab that pivots open to reveal a courtyard (right) centered on a reflecting basin.*

studied in the three dimensions. But it is the site itself that usually sparks the ideas. Cunningham makes many return visits after the initial sketches and their subsequent development to test the design against the reality of the site.

For Harmony, the five-foot-eight-inch Cunningham touchingly walked the site with a platform box to simulate the height of his six-foot-two-inch client—to see what he would see. The architect was organizing rooms and calibrating view corridors with strings to understand how the house would frame the landscape for which the owners had come. Like a nineteenth-century landscape artist, Cunningham was composing views, using beams, columns, and the volume of rooms as the bracketing devices.

But besides pursuing a picturesque tradition in architecture, Cunningham was implementing a design attitude that implies architecture understood as experience rather than concept. Cunningham wanted to deliver the landscape to the corridors, couches, and dining tables where the clients would be spending their day: He felt that the views should engage them directly, actively forming and informing their daily environment with an almost physical immediacy. "They bought the house for the view,

Light creates three-dimensional compositions of walls, beams, and skylights in the living room (left) and in the guest bedroom corridor, exercise room, and kitchen (right).

that's what they paid for, and I wanted to be sure they had it," he says with his customary matter-of-factness. The house did not grow out of the site in a Wrightian sense, emerging from the ground organically with sliding horizontal walls. It grew instead once removed from the landscape, from the sight lines which would deliver the view inside with a palpable impact. The openness of the house absorbed the views integrally, making them environmental rather than more distantly pictorial. The clients occupy the view because of a heightened sensuous awareness provoked by the house.

To elevate the house into the view, and to best position its occupants, Cunningham sculpted the earth into a plinth that circumscribed the house, defining its occupiable precinct within a much larger piece of property. Cunningham customarily extrapolates parts of the house into the landscape, shaping land forms, and during his site visits, he realized he could edit out neighboring houses in the foreground simply by building retaining walls that cropped out the structures, creating the illusion that the house had few if any immediate neighbors. Channeling long views as it edited the foreground, the house

The owner wished to live outside; the bedroom (left) is actually an exterior enclosed by glass. The waterfall (right) appears from nowhere; when it's not flowing, it disappears.

emerged as an optical instrument, much like Sea View in San Clemente, but on a larger scale. A crescent-shaped swimming pool at the front of the house formed part of the editing process, as it changed the subject: The surfaces reflect the sky as the infinity edge melts into the horizon.

Cunningham was able to adapt in La Jolla to the tight confines of an urban lot, and here the architect encountered the opposite problem—a sprawling site within a huge panorama. But even a 10,000-square-foot house could appear insignificant in a landscape this open and large. Cunningham, like most architects affected by Wright, breaks the box. In Harmony, as this house came to be called, the architect decided to expand the box as he broke it, to give the building a scale commensurate with the acreage surrounding it and the landscape beyond, to which it visually belongs.

Outdoor spaces inside the house pressure the perimeter, pushing it out. The onyx front door opens to a spacious entry court centered on a reflecting pool, minimally landscaped with three trees—a redbud and a red and a green Japanese maple—that recall the owners' sojourn in Japan. A wide sheet of water cascades into the pool from a long projecting beam, a Barraganesque touch, but one with a purpose here: "My clients told stories about the waterfalls in South Africa and the long eaves of their traditional house in Japan," says Cunningham. A rock garden, which the architect frequently rakes himself into liquid patterns, is set within the master bedroom area, separating the bedroom itself from the baths and home gym. Cunningham expands the house from within with the matrix of yards as seen in The Arbors.

The perimeter of the house is stepped and involuted in ways that invite the landscape into the occupied area. Cunningham also extends the house into the yard with deep overhead trellises that act as outriggers claiming an additional 10,000 square feet of outside territory for the house. The trellises form shaded, generously sized exterior spaces where the couple can live and entertain en pleine aire. The husband lived in South Africa when he was a boy, and felt comfortable living in big, outdoor areas. Space in this house is biographical. Cunningham built memory.

Because his clients wanted to bring the feeling of outdoor living inside, Cunningham created a three-dimensional construction system that stacks like cards. The trellises, long fins set on end, continue inside where they are sometimes stacked two or three levels high: The slots between the fins are glazed so that what seems like a lattice open to the sky functions as a roof. Similarly, the walls are broken into stepped piers, the gaps between them glazed.

The result is a porous fabric of beams and piers

weaving over and under each other, all positioned within a circular landform that Cunningham inscribes, like an earthwork, around the architectural compound. "It's like a great spiderweb or lacework expanded across site," he says. "It is not an object." As at Cityhouse, the structure, though orthogonal, is not static but sets up dynamic circulation patterns. The piers step diagonally across the house and site, creating diagonal vectors leading through the house.

As at Cityhouse, sunlight and moonlight penetrate the slotted openings, creating gyroscopic patterns of turning light. "The house is not the solid; the shadows are, and otherwise the house dissolves in the luminosity. Just how the grid plays itself out and projects light is not predictable, but separating and layering the parts allowed me to produce an intangible and ethereal space that always defers to the view."

Rather than designing volumes sculpted by the sun, as Le Corbusier advocated, Cunningham weaves a structural web of beams and columns that filters the sun.

Left: *Beams are visually completed in the pool, becoming an object bracketing space and its reflection.* Right: *A fireplace with a glass roof separates public and private spaces.* Following pages: *Evening at the guest wings and breakfast wing.*

Corbusier was influenced by the solid volumes of masonry architecture of the Mediterranean; Cunningham was interested instead in the grape arbors that sheltered people from the same sun. He designed Harmony to allow the building to reveal light as a phenomenon, and not the light to feature the building—he was more interested in the sunbeams than the beams. A house with so much covered space would normally suffer from gloomy interiors, but the trellis allows balanced daylighting throughout the interiors rather than intense natural light at the perimeter, which rapidly falls off inside. "The shadows stretch across the whole interior," he says. "It's like standing under a tree with large leaves—you get these beautiful sunbeams moving through the building, not just light from the sides. It's a spatial apparatus that acts as a time machine light filter."

In his emphasis on light, with a building oriented to the sky, Cunningham virtually overlooks the earth, and therefore distances himself again from his Taliesin roots: As in Cityhouse, he is stretching beyond his formative influences toward other elemental paradigms.

Unlike landscapes like New England's, which are intimate, the West is penetrated by a sense of vastness, particularly in the arid areas of inland San Diego, and the porosity of the house as an expanded fabric not only captures the pervasive feeling of grandeur in this part of

tectural possibilities even in communities with tightly pre-scribed design guidelines.

In an architecturally homogenous enclave of San Diego with another design review board, virtually every house on the curving blocks looks like an ersatz hacien-da shortchanged of its ranch. In a commission for Alice and Arthur Kramer, Cunningham looked to the work of Modernist San Diego pioneer Irving Gill, who brought the undecorated wall to a point of Platonic simplicity. Cunningham was interested in the power of Gill's walls to give strong definition to architectural volumes and outdoor spaces. The wall—plain, undecorated, punctured with windows only occasionally—has remained a major element in Cunningham's repertoire of forms because its space-defining powers allow him spatial control.

Adapting Gill's idiom, Cunningham reinvented the usual plan typology for houses at The Arbors, designing a house dispersed over a "field" rather than configured as an object. Cunningham parsed major and minor courtyards, most centered on a water feature, through a house that, with its wings, expanded across the full yard. In a highly civilized interpretation of California living, the architect creat-ed a matrix of indoor and outdoor spaces that pattern the site in an expanded grid. With broad sliding doors inset within the otherwise uninterrupted walls, the dom-inantly one-story house is highly porous, and its flexible

Southern California, but also, by reference, the grandeur of the veldts of South Africa. The expanded fabric, how-ever, also cultivates the more ephemeral aspects of an environment in which light itself, through its intensity, chal-lenges and even dissolves matter: The porosity of the structure admits light patterns that dematerialize the structure. Though he is working as a Romantic shaping picturesque compositions, Cunningham is also construct-ing, like an Impressionist, a three-dimensional architectural painting out of the effects of light.

The architect is pursuing difficult aesthetic goals by using the elements themselves—light, space, sky, and water—to define the essential qualities of the house. Harmony is a seasoned and synoptic work in an artisti-cally ambitious career that was shifting focus from the material to the immaterial.

THE ARBORS   After fifteen years of practice in privi-leged arenas of San Diego that offered him the kind of commissions that supported experimentation, Cunningham had collected a portfolio of projects, both built and unbuilt, that prepared him to expand the archi-

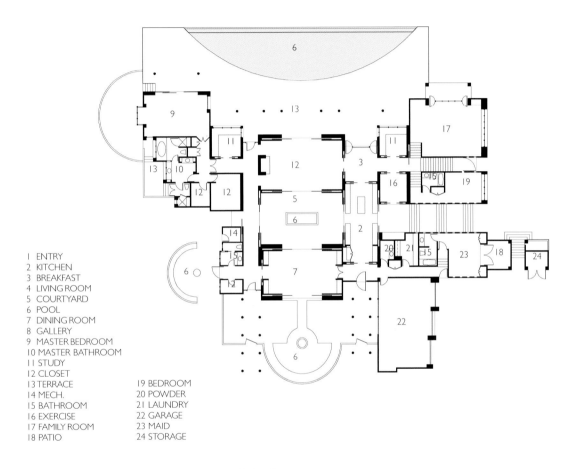

1 ENTRY
2 KITCHEN
3 BREAKFAST
4 LIVING ROOM
5 COURTYARD
6 POOL
7 DINING ROOM
8 GALLERY
9 MASTER BEDROOM
10 MASTER BATHROOM
11 STUDY
12 CLOSET
13 TERRACE
14 MECH.
15 BATHROOM
16 EXERCISE
17 FAMILY ROOM
18 PATIO

19 BEDROOM
20 POWDER
21 LAUNDRY
22 GARAGE
23 MAID
24 STORAGE

Opposite: *Cunningham layers space with an enfilade of doorways that lead from an entry court to a central courtyard to the pool terrace overlooking the long view.*

Above right: *The view of the pool from the terrace.*

nature takes on a character determined by its use: The house field reverses, the courtyard becoming living and dining rooms during outdoor soirées, for example, as the furnished areas take on supporting background roles.

Cunningham here carried over his insights from Cityhouse to another flat site limited in acreage. On the view side of the house, the architect may pay due respect to the golf course immediately opposite the living room with a bank of sliding glass walls, but overall he devises an ingeniously internalized plan that checkers the entire property, giving value to areas away from the main event. The indoor-outdoor plan, with pocket gardens adjacent to the wings, creates chiaroscuro patterns of light that recall those at Cityhouse, but at a larger scale: Light here comes not in striations but in blocks filling the courtyard volumes. Cunningham's creative resistance to rules yielded an unexpected, highly livable new organization for the house.

RAY Cunningham's commissions seem to alternate between the wide open spaces near Rancho Santa Fe and the more constricted lots of the beach communities like La Jolla. Each of the two types of commissions makes different kinds of strategic demands on the architect, but the beach properties are inherently more limiting and challenging. In 1999 Cunningham started the design of a house for another retired couple, on a hillside overlooking the ocean in La Jolla. The property was located on a suburban street where houses were designed according to the convention of placing the house between a picturesquely planted front yard and a more recreational backyard. The house, regardless of its style or floor plan, stands behind a facade that projects the dominant image of a building that also acts as a fence, protecting the backyard's privacy. Cunningham's houses exhibit the same independence within their community that he has always exhibited personally, whether at Taliesin or any other structured environment. In La Jolla, he saw no reason to bond with the

Left: *The ceiling of the skylight and the curvature of the staircase leading to it.* Right: *The continuous glass wall on the viewside of the house, with all rooms facing the ocean panorama. The curve of the roofs opens to the view in a sweeping gesture.*

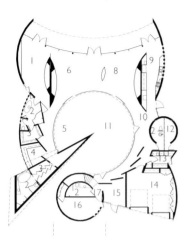

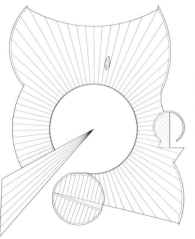

1 MASTER BEDROOM
2 BATHROOM
3 WARDROBE
4 OFFICE
5 HALL GALLERY
6 LIVING ROOM
7 FIREPLACE
8 DINING ROOM
9 KITCHEN
10 PANTRY
11 COURTYARD
12 GARDEN
13 LAUNDRY
14 GARAGE
15 STUDY
16 BEDROOM
17 CLOSET
18 STUDIO

LOWER LEVEL PLAN, STUDIO PLAN, ROOF PLAN

houses of an architecturally weak neighborhood in polite gestures of agreement, but preferred instead to create a separate world. He does not accept the received wisdom of the suburban house typology of a house centered on a lot.

Above: *The roofscape, showing courtyards and roof panels radiating from it. The tower on the left is the painting studio; the spiral on the right is the glass-ceilinged powder room. Opposite left: The living room, courtyard, and garden.*

Even at Cityhouse on his first lot in La Jolla, which was so narrow that a townhouse would have been an obvious design answer, Cunningham avoided the presumed typology. Again in La Jolla, on a wider more suburban lot, Cunningham eschewed established precedent. Rather than assuming a one-story box, the architect exploded the box from the interior of the lot with a courtyard that pushed the rooms to the perimeter of the site. As at Cityhouse, the yard occupied the center, although here the house formed a nearly complete circle around the yard, with a standing-seam copper roof inclined toward the yard like an impluvium. The roof starts low at the front of the house, and then rises in the living and dining rooms at the rear, releasing the occupants to the view through a dramatically tall wall of glass under an arcuated roof that frames the view. A koi pond lies just beyond the glass before the hillside drops down the slope. The house uses the whole site, appropriating and internalizing outdoor space as a landscaped room. The house seems to expand within its own boundaries even before it borrows the view of the

The cantilevered fireplace divides the living room and dining space and provides structural support for the roof. A continuous glass wall divides interior and exterior; the curved ceiling thrusts up toward the view of sky and ocean.

ocean. The circularity of the plan keeps the eye turning, augmenting the illusion of spatial generosity.

CRESCENT   Another site up the coast in Encinitas was far easier by comparison because the 7,000-square-foot program for a pair of empty-nesters was smaller relative to the area of buildable land. Still, the ocean-front lot was not large, and the size limitations of the site prompted Cunningham to again design a house that would construct the site and expand it in the vertical dimension: Elevating the house to maximize the water view required stacking the building. Again, because the upper floor presented a superior view, Cunningham inverted floors, placing the more public spaces that would be used daily—the kitchen, living and dining areas, and the master bedroom—on the third floor. The garages and service areas occupied the ground floor, and guest rooms for visiting children and grandchildren, with separate entrances, the second floor.

Left: *Overhanging roof seen against the sky.* Right: *The powder room has a solid granite basin, glass ceilings, and glass wall.* Opposite right: *Looking skyward through powder room. The glass celing is supported by a steel tube.* Far right: *Stainless steel cables form a virtual corner to the volume of the house at the property line.*

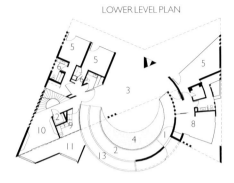

LOWER LEVEL PLAN

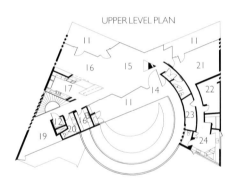

UPPER LEVEL PLAN

1 ENTRY GATE
2 RAMP UP TO TERRACE
3 BREEZEWAY
4 POOL
5 BEDROOM
6 BATH
7 CLOSET
8 EXERCISE ROOM
9 LAUNDRY
10 OFFICE
11 TERRACE
12 ELEVATOR
13 RAMP UP TO UPPER LEVEL
14 ENTRY
15 LIVING ROOM
16 DINING ROOM
17 KITCHEN
18 PANTRY
19 TV ROOM
20 POWDER ROOM
21 MASTER BEDROOM
22 HER WARDROBE
23 HIS WARDROBE
24 MASTER BATH

The architectural modesty of Encinitas streets on bluffs running parallel to the beach below belies the grandeur of the ocean, the sky, and horizon just on the far side of the front-row houses. Designing the house to condition the visitors and owners psychologically for the spectacle to come, the architect conceived the house as a foil to the ocean and sky beyond. Cunningham cultivates anticipation by starting visitors along a circular ramp that submits them to a suspenseful buildup. Cunningham slows space by parsing out the entry; the meditative procession acts as a delay into the building.

Guests park behind a tall hedge of bamboo, the first buffer zone into the house. They approach a front door that opens into an exterior entry court. As at the Brushstroke, the visit unfolds as guests start up a ramp that edges past a crescent-shaped pool. Just after the start of the promenade, their eyes rise to the level of the water pooled in the black-bottomed basin, and when

Spiral circulation ramp in concrete and glass, around the crescent-shaped swimming pool. The entry ramps act as a wall between the garden and driveway. Crossed by a curving line, this large, pivoting stainless-steel gate to the courtyard reinforces the shapes of the crescent-shaped pool and circular ramps beyond the door. The door's handle is in a pocket of this curve.

they look out across the water to the horizon, the surface of the water in the pool merges with the surfaces of the ocean water in the kind of ethereal experience around which Cunningham increasingly plans his projects. Poetically, the two sheets of water, sweet and salty, are continuous (as at Louis Kahn's Salk Institute, where the stream appears to fill the ocean beyond the plaza).

Mid-level, at the second floor landing, a disc-shaped concrete terrace fits into the hollow of the crescent pool. The terrace here, bridged overhead by the elevated third floor, frames a view of the yard and a glimpse of the ocean beyond.

Cunningham switches the direction of the circulation, for a certain back-and-forth inefficiency that lengthens the promenade, heightening the anticipation. The path proceeds up another ramp of wider circumference, creating the illusion of greater distance and the need for more time. The ramp leads to a landing on the third floor,

Left: *This terrace acts as an island between the house and the pool. Reflections in the pool bring the sky down onto the ground plan. Guests entering the house first walk beneath this plane and then break above its surface as they rise on the ramp to the garden level.* Right: *The viewside of the house, with the terrace in the foreground.* Following pages: *Dining room and living room.*

where the expansive living spaces front the entire width of the property and offer an unobstructed view to the ocean panorama, through a long wall of plate glass. Cunningham has choreographed a rich spatial sequence that spins visitors on a dance through highly sculpted volumes. He deploys the volumes to edit out the buildings to the side, to focus on the ocean in front, and deftly juxtaposes raw concrete to the ether beyond. In the living room, he introduces a new, angular geometry that creates a spatial diagonal thrust across the living area: The ceiling, which rises as it angles out to the ocean, helps shoot the eye out to infinity. Cunningham has used the volumes to create solids and voids that spatialize the

A skylight runs through the building, casting patterns of sunlight, right, on the walls and floors. The master bedroom (above) is a simple space facing a plate-glass view of the ocean.

house three-dimensionally, and the circling and angling geometries dynamize the space. "I wanted to expand the sense of space even though it was a city lot," he says.

The house is not so much a formal object as it is a three-dimensional armature that leads occupants through and to constructed outdoor open spaces, especially the large patio terrace and the expansive balcony above. The architect takes a holistic view of the entire site, giving emphatic value to the third dimension through development of the cross section. Cunningham designs a spatially rich section where circular, orthogonal, and diagonal geometries overlap. The house is not a passive passageway into the view, but a design that contextualizes the ocean in a spatially dynamic frame. Cunningham has scripted a visual narrative for how to see the ocean.

RAZOR BLUFF   Instead of being simply small, the difficulty presented by another property in La Jolla, near the Salk Institute, was that it was nearly impossible to build.

A stainless-steel-and-glass staircase supported by a central tube with cantilevered treads create kaleidoscopic patterns of light mixing with silhouette. Above this staircase is the narrow end of the triangular skylight that runs through the house. Following pages: Looking to infinity: The roofscape shows the network of zig-zagging structural beams.

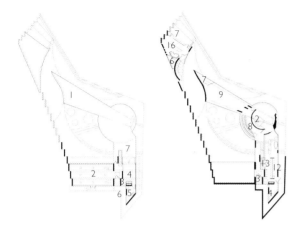

1 ENTRY
2 EXERCISE ROOM
3 ELEVATOR
4 BEDROOM
5 BATH
6. GARDEN
7. ROOF TERRACE
8. BALCONY
9. SITTING ROOM
10. MASTER BED

11. MASTER BATH
12. HIS WARDROBE
13. HER WARDROBE
14. SHOWER/STEAM
15. LIGHT WELL
16. OFFICE
17. LIVING ROOM
18. DINING ROOM
19. KITCHEN
20. POWDER ROOM

Previous pages, left and right: *Construction images of Razor Bluff. The bluff on which this house is built is like a great geological island, and the house extends the illusion of an island. The house is built of poured-in-place white Portland cement that gives the appearance of a pure, white marble.*

There was no received wisdom for how to handle the site, which had already been abandoned by several other owners and architects. Cunningham decided to collapse the site and the house into the same design, so that the house forms the site infrastructure and vice versa. Cunningham would virtually build the site by building the house.

Designers of many other houses in this exclusive neighborhood imported styles from different continents and eras, but Cunningham, even if he wanted to adopt a style, could not because the functional demands on the house, including the vertical packing, determined the design as a feat of site organization and engineering. The amount of infrastructural work required by the site amounted to that of a small bridge. The house was conceived as occupied structure.

Cunningham, first of all, assumed the boundaries allowed by the Coastal Commission, which basically determined the permissible volume: A conventional suburban house couldn't be planted here on a level podium

Right: *A glass room forms a bridge above the roof terrace.* Left: *The pool blends with the ocean.* Pages 126-129: *Architectural elements, from stair treads to curved walls, become sculptural elements of the abstract architectural composition.*

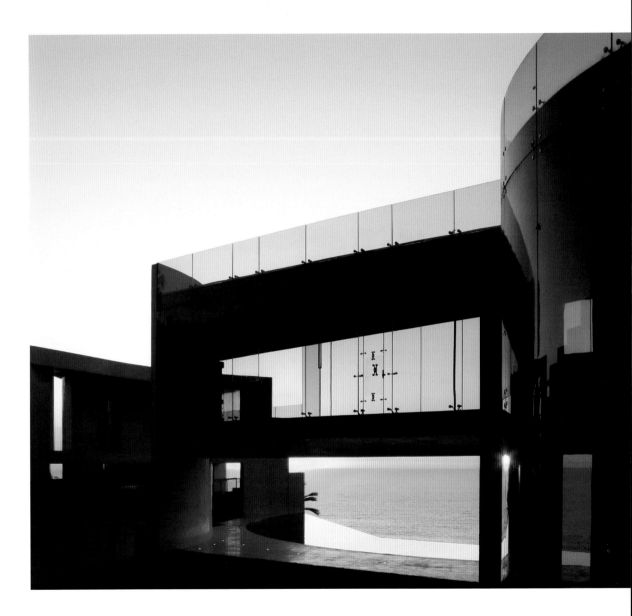

RAZOR BLUFF

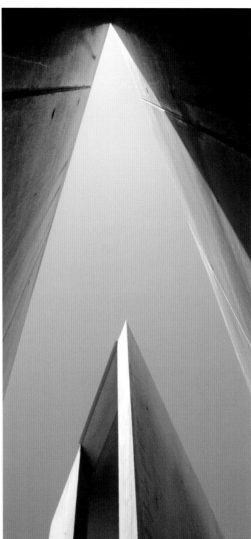
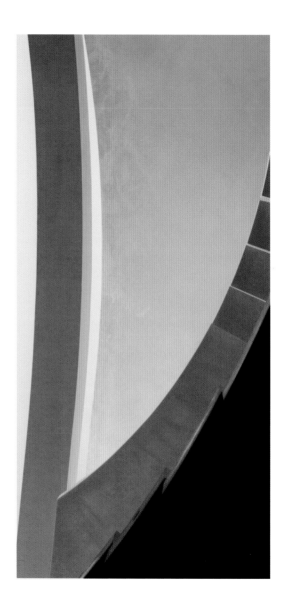

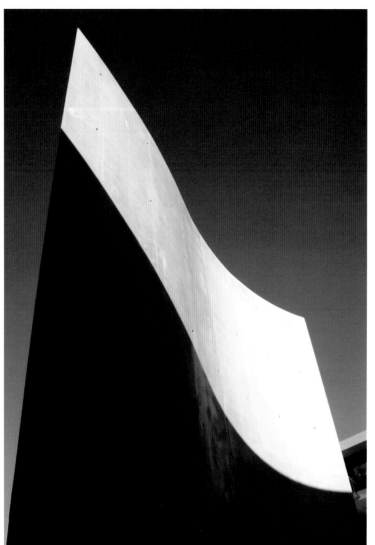

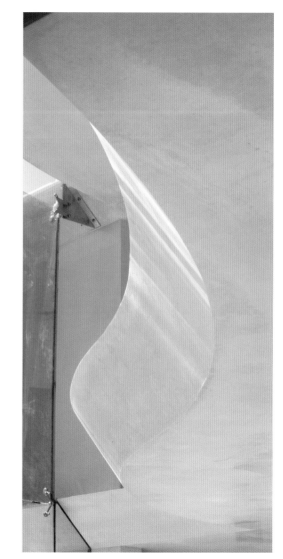

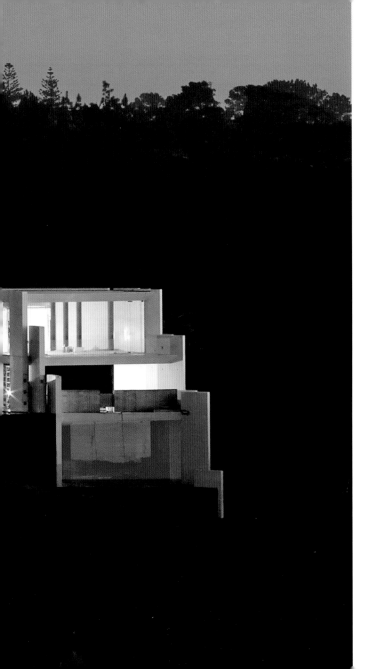

because siting a large house on the limited amount of land basically required what Cunningham describes as "a multi-level cliff dwelling." Building the house toward the view necessitated a deep retaining wall on the uphill slope, against which Cunningham would nest the three-story structure. Cunningham wanted the house to step down the slope so that each roof formed a terrace to the adjacent upper floor, recreating the outdoor space that the house itself displaced. As usual, the architect used structural elements of the house to frame desired views, determining what he wanted, and did not want, to see. The architect hollowed out the interior, creating a perimeter house wrapped around an open courtyard, permitting daylight into rooms adjacent to the retaining wall.

Cunningham came to the project prepared by his designs for other commissions in which he had pursued similar strategies. In most, he abandoned the convention of the house conceived as a stand-alone object in favor of an uncentered building dispersed to the perimeter of a site redefined as an occupied field. At Razor Bluff, the field became three dimensional, extending several stories below the original surface.

Left: *Stem to stern, the full house, shot at dusk.*
Right: *The living room and master bedroom are reflected in the carved-out shape of the swimming pool.*

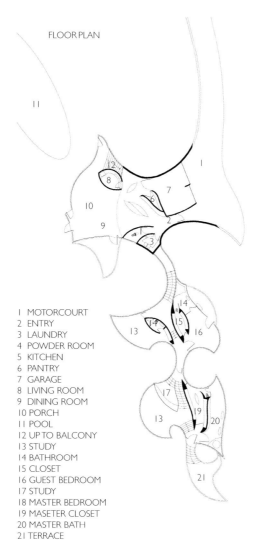

FLOOR PLAN

11

12
8
10
7
6
9
2
3

14
14 15
13   16

17
13   19
20

21

1 MOTORCOURT
2 ENTRY
3 LAUNDRY
4 POWDER ROOM
5 KITCHEN
6 PANTRY
7 GARAGE
8 LIVING ROOM
9 DINING ROOM
10 PORCH
11 POOL
12 UP TO BALCONY
13 STUDY
14 BATHROOM
15 CLOSET
16 GUEST BEDROOM
17 STUDY
18 MASTER BEDROOM
19 MASETER CLOSET
20 MASTER BATH
21 TERRACE

VOLER If his series of metaphoric buildings marked a period of conceptual growth when Cunningham opened his designs to a highly expressive range, a recent project, yet unbuilt, promises to be the start of another series establishing a new direction.

The commission started as a critique. Pascal Brandys, a genetic engineer and recreational helicopter pilot, had spotted and admired one of Cunningham's houses from the air, but while he thought it unusual in the context of other houses in the aerial view, he still found it conservative: The client noted that it relied too much on regular geometry. In his helicopter peregrinations, the client had also found and bought a spectacular mountaintop site, with craggy granitic outcroppings and an inland view of Lake Hodges. Brandys wanted to site a house in this untouched wilderness, but did not want geometry to tame it. "Usually I'm the one challenging the clients," says Cunningham, "but Pascal pushed me, and opened up my design."

After the ground was cleared of brush, the pines were surveyed and plotted by computer, and a topographic map completed. The architect walked the site,

Preceding pages: Voler's model, over a photograph of its site. Left and right: The titanium roof, modeled in lead, gives the impression of helicopter blades glinting in the light.

and based on the views and the quality of the outcroppings, determined the area that was suitable for a structure. The site suggested the house could not be a solid: The outcroppings were the salient feature of the site, and bringing them out individually necessitated fragmenting the house and nesting the rooms in their interstices. Cunningham realized that the fragmentary nature of the architecture created the possibility of the house itself becoming a feature of the landscape, and that parts of the house could look back on other sections, forming part of the larger view. Closely associated with the rocks, the house could become the subject of its own contemplation.

After laying out rooms on the ground between outcroppings, he devised an elevated pathway among the ridges, starting at the most public part of the house and leading to the most private. Occupants will drop down from the path to the rooms through the individual rocks.

Since the client will often fly into and off the site, Cunningham designed the roof to act as a facade. Cunningham wanted to capture some sense of rotating movement, recalling helicopter blades, but also he hybridized the forms with the idea of giant fabric floating in the breeze over the rocks. Columns supporting the roofs were all angled, to accentuate the dynamism of the roof's movement.

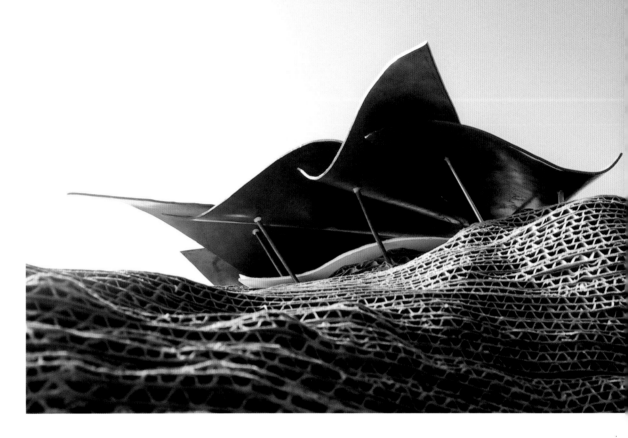

For a client who lives in the air, Cunningham created an architecture of the air—windblown and propelled. Without being literally mimetic of the landscape's wildness, Cunningham has not just relaxed his geometries but applied complexity and chaos theory to create a house predicated on an image of air turbulence. Cunningham's architecture remained elemental. He had simply chosen another element, and interpreted it in a particular aerodynamic state.

PUBLIC BUILDINGS

LA ATALLAYA   For the eastern slope of a hillside planted with an olive grove, on an estate adjacent to one of
the great lagoons and nature preserves in San Diego,
Cunningham designed a private art gallery and car museum. The building would also serve for entertaining and as
the daytime offices for the estate.

Longitudinal sections form phantom perspectives, part visible,
part implied. These illustrations show the structural skeleton
and the three-dimensional volume of space it creates.

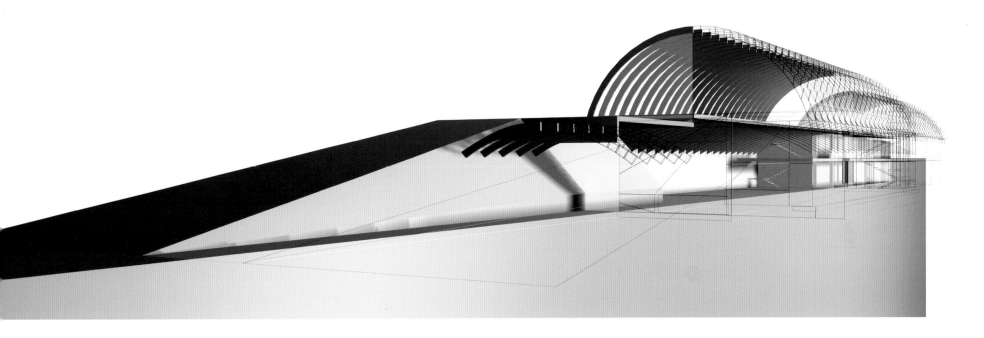

Always sensitive to the land, Cunningham decided, as he says, "to touch the land as minimally as possible," and also to echo two rural building traditions in California, the greenhouses used for raising flowers, and the virtually extinct Quonset hut, a vaulted structure made of galvanized metal. To minimize the footprint, Cunningham proposed building two-thirds of the square footage underground beneath a semicircular glass vault structured with large steel ribs. The car museum would be located at grade within the greenhouse, and the art, more sensitive to light, would occupy an open, double-height, column-free space two floors below. Staircases and an elevator would lead downstairs to a mezzanine level overlooking the double-height gallery space, planned as a multipurpose room that could be used for lectures and entertainment as well as for art display. The offices surrounded an open court at one end of the structure. Cunningham carved a drive into the lowest level, berming the embankments with angular inclines, sculpting an earthwork leading into the base of the structure. Cunningham, here, was not building a structure so much as shaping light, the clay of any gallery.

The only part of the structure visible was the rib cage, sitting at grade like a Quonset hut. The ribs established the rhythm of the structure, but Cunningham softened the shadow patterns through the ribs with translucent glazing, which would haze the light coming in during the day, and cause the structure to glow at night. The floor of the first story, intended for the car museum, was also built in translucent glass, so that the light that had filtered through the ribbed glass vault was filtered again as it fell, very gently, to the gallery below. By the time it arrived at the paintings, brushing their surfaces, the light was soft

almost not there—not only because of treading lightly on the land, but also because of his concern that the building not overshadow the art. "The evenness of the structure would give a quietness to the space," he says. The architect who says he tries to create buildings as works of art holds back in deference to the art, or rather, transforms the act of shaping raw matter into the art of constructing light. He is practicing as a space-and-light artist in the tradition of Robert Irwin.

OCEANSIDE MUSEUM OF ART   Traditionally, architects build their practices up from domestic work, but the transition from houses to institutions is always difficult. Cunningham nearly made the leap when he was short-listed for the design of a local museum in Oceanside. Cunningham finally did not win, but since many of his homes verge on an institutional scale, he easily made the transition in terms of design, applying the expertise and insight he had acquired over twenty-five years of practice.

The commission for the Oceanside Museum of Art involved adding an extension onto existing structures, including a historic building by Irving Gill. Cunningham's unique insight about structuring the site with a building served the program well here. Avoiding the concept of the museum as a simple, freestanding object, the architect

and protective, screened by two layers of high-performance glass.

Cunningham here was constructing light. First, he filtered it, and changed its quality from harsh to gentle— "so that light blushes, varying between a soft shadow and a soft light so different from Southern California shadow patterns." The intention, says Cunningham, was to create

The Oceanside Museum was designed to be a lantern in the night sky.

an environmental kaleidoscope that would change with the angle of the sun during the day and through the seasons of the year. Cunningham underscored the variation in the light by keeping the long, tunneling structure clear and simple, so the shifts are legible against a clean, simple background. He proposed sandblasting the glass, which effectively sculpts the surface of the glass three dimensionally, producing the unusual specular effect of radiating light in all directions. The treatment heightens the luminosity.

Cunningham wanted the structure to be so simple—

proposed perimeter structures that formed a civic court-yard at the center of the full-block site, a space usable for outdoor performances and exhibitions. He bridges the edge of the civic space with an elevated structure that, while serving as a gallery, connects the far two sides of the site. Forms are simple and direct, but the strategy of deploying the additions to create outdoor cultural space extroverts a building type that is normally closed and internalized. The architect applies his practice of dispersing and spatializing structures within a porous three-dimensional field.

MUSEUM FOR JAPANESE ART AND CULTURE   The museum commission that eluded him in nearby Oceanside came, instead, in the form of a commission to design the Japan Center in the Central Valley. Unexpectedly, Cunningham met Mr. and Mrs. Willard Clark, collectors of Asian art who asked the San Diegan to design a combination museum/*kunsthalle* for exhibiting a very personal and distinguished collection of mostly Japanese artifacts ranging from precious kimonos to rare screens and block prints. The collection had traveled to Japan, where it was both a critical and popular success. It was recognized and hailed as the largest return of Japanese art in the history of the country. Mr. Clark had been stationed in Japan after World War II, when he fell in love with the art and culture. With the curatorial advice of Sherman Lee, former director of the Cleveland Museum of Art, he amassed a large, eclectic collection over a half century. The Clarks built a small private gallery for the works, which has proved too small for the still growing collection. The couple needed a larger venue with a presence commensurate with the stature of the collection, a building that could also serve as a cultural center for Japanese Americans and for Japan. He decided against locating the museum in one of the coastal cities, which are already served by Asian museums, choosing their homestead in the Central Valley, which has its own history of Japanese American immigration and settlement. The museum would be sited on a flat parcel of land set within a walnut grove on the couple's ranch.

When they met, the Clarks had already conceived the project as a copy of a temple, and he asked Cunningham to comment on his design. Cunningham felt that, as an imitation, the temple was too obvious. "It wasn't triggering memory, so its value was questionable," he recalls. "I thought the integrity of the culture and art pointed in another direction." The Clarks asked him what he would do.

As always, Cunningham looked to the landscape to understand the nature of the commission, and in the flat Central Valley, he was struck by the canals coursing through the fields and orchards, "these flat ribbons of silver running through the land," the architect notes. He decided to play on the theme of water by expanding the canal into a reflecting basin, where he would plant the building, an island in an inland sea designed with an infinity edge. The building would be seen from all sides, dimensionalized in its own upside-down reflection.

Cunningham has conceived allusive architecture before, as in the Saltman house, where the ancient timber columns supported an inverted vaulted roof, and—without being imitative—somehow recalled Asian temples. In the context of the commission for the Japan center, Cunningham decided to allude to the source of the collection by reinterpreting traditional Japanese architecture. For climatic reasons, he would work in steel rather than wood, while maintaining the idea of a skeletal frame.

"It would have been easy to buy and import old Japanese buildings, but I translated the wood into steel because of the cycles of dryness and wet in the Central Valley," says Cunningham. "The wood would have dried out and twisted, and created a maintenance nightmare."

Frank Lloyd Wright took inspiration from Japanese buildings, which he famously reinterpreted into a signature style. Cunningham reinterprets the same tradition differently. The building that will be rising in a serene reflecting basin, set within the quiet of the grove, is clear-

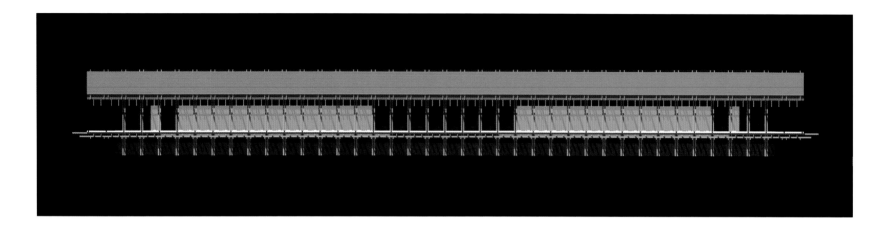

ly inspired by the typology of the Japanese temple, and beyond that, by very ancient traditions of longhouses built in the Pacific, with tree trunks elevating living quarters above the humidity of the ground. Cunningham has not made any specific historic reference but has recast this essential idea for a different time and place.

The basic elements of this kind of structure are the columns, which support a living podium sheltered by a massive roof that acts as both an umbrella and parasol. The enclosures are basically nonstructural infills—the shoji screens in Japanese houses—set between the columns and within the structure as panels, which may easily be changed and moved.

As for many Modernists, the plan is the generator of the building, and Cunningham conceived for this clear skeletal structure a straightforward plan on two floors. Visitors enter the long, relatively narrow structure over a bridge leading to the middle of the right side, where the building receives them with a two-story atrium reception area flanked by a set of galleries. As in a traditional building, visitors remove their shoes. The rest of the floor at this level, floating just above the water level, is devoted to offices. The orthogonal layout inside, both in the offices and galleries, takes its geometric cue from the orthogonal structure of the defining framework.

From the reception area, visitors move up a pair of stairs to the main gallery, where exhibitions will be arrayed in a long open space under the roof, whose framing is exposed. Perimeter walls are formed by movable panels set against the glass in the space between the columns. Shows can be designed in the column-free space as the exhibits suggest and require. Natural light filters over the top of the display walls into the galleries.

Cunningham is never a literalist, and in a building explicitly rooted in a foreign tradition, he reinvents the givens, starting with the structure. By using steel rather than wood, he avoids many of the constraints that Japanese builders had to respect. Because he does not have to protect the Cor-Ten steel he is specifying from the sun and rain (he wants it to rust and age) as he would timber, he can project the roof structure beyond the roof, and liberate the roof supports from the roof they support.

Starting with the perimeter, he quadruples the columns, introducing in the slots between the paired sets of columns a scale of intimate space within this normally heroic type of structure. The columns themselves, made of four rather than one member, are more fragile.

"Every piece is separate and clearly expressed, one atop the other, without intersections," he says. "The idea was to maintain the integrity of every member; the clarity came from traditional architecture." The steel construction allows him to project the weave well beyond the edge of the roof, so that it cantilevers past the body of the building, hovering acrobatically in pure space, where the California light takes hold, casting the members in chiaroscuro, projecting gridded shadows onto the water below. "In Japanese architecture, the members don't protrude, but here, the light is so intense, I wanted to capture the pattern projected through the structure."

The building embodies a Japanese sensibility at many levels. Beyond the clarity, and the exquisite sense of order, what is Japanese about the design is the integrity of shapes and forms—the long gallery shape, the prominence of the roof, the regularity of structure, the stacking of members. All trigger memory, as Cunningham says, in what emerges as a generalized after-image of Japanese

This museum reinterprets ancient Japanese temples and, without being imitative or literal about precedent, triggers associations in memory.

architecture without reference to a specific historical name and place.

But beyond distilling a tradition, he evokes the magic that haunts those buildings by conjuring the sensations they evoke—qualities of reflection, light and shade, and stillness in which the ethereal appears and prospers. Even the light striking the dark, rich, rusted surface of the Cor-Ten produces a golden glow all the more magical when mirrored on the plane of the water. "We wanted this golden glow to the building, like a golden pavilion in the water."

No single ephemeral effect dominates the environment. They all wax and wane on their own, and mix in ever-shifting drifts of change. Cunningham has orchestrated a building that sets up the conditions for these effects, touching them off, creating a subtext of ephemera all the more fragile within the framework of a robust steel structure. "In Japanese art, the closer you look, the finer it is." As always, Cunningham pursues intangibility, and the pursuit is especially appropriate in the context of a culture that has always praised shadows.

Practicing outside any "ism," with only nine months of architectural apprenticeship under his belt, Cunningham has shepherded his own development on a house-by-house basis. From a mother sensitive to the arts, the patrons who befriended him, and mentors like de Czarnecka, he learned to look at all the arts in general as part of a comprehensive way of seeing and understanding the world. This deeply ingrained cultural receptivity opened him to many influences, from the Frank Lloyd Wright houses in Chicago, to the Modernist sculpture he saw at The Art Institute of Chicago and the Japanese prints and Asian artifacts at Taliesin, to the jazz clubs of San Diego. The lesson he took into the rolling hills of Rancho Santa Fe was that architecture was an art, and that he would practice as an artist. In the context of the late 1970s, as other architects challenged modernism by advocating forays into architectural history, his position was rare, fresh, and even daring. Designed in 1979 and finished in 1982, Wing House represented a highly original response and alternative to the polarizing Modernist–Postmodernist style wars then raging. Wing House was an inspired design carried off with a maturity remarkable for an architect in his mid twenties.

Cunningham says that he would prefer not to deal with gravity and site, that he would prefer to do "absolute art," but in the mix of artistic impulse and functional program, a lyricism always transcends the functionalism. Some of the designs are based on repetition of strict geometric forms developed in regular progression. In other examples, the geometry is freer and more metaphoric. In most of the projects, he fuses form and structure in a seamless synthesis of architecture and engineering that reinforces rather than subordinates the poetic impulse. Whereas Modernists often expose supporting systems as a building theme, and often even feature structure as the basis of architectonic aesthetic and meaning, Cunningham subordinates structure and mechanics to the overriding poetic idea. In most of his buildings, he expresses motion as a point of departure, so highlighting notions of support and joinery would be counterproductive because they emphasize fixity rather than flow and flight. The buildings do not focus on their own instrumentality as their subject, as in many high tech buildings; Cunningham subordinates technique to effect.

John Lautner, with whom Cunningham occasionally visited in Los Angeles, once said that Mexican architects were not—like their American counterparts—afraid of architecture. The observation was as much a comment about Lautner's own daring work as it was an appreciation of Mexican architecture. Cunningham, familiar with Lautner's opus, displays the same fearlessness, and if he does not practice "absolute art," he strives for what he calls "absolute architecture." At the back of Harmony, a building that articulates the panorama and invites in the elements through a strong formal idea, Cunningham places a lone, freestanding column that has no purpose other than its own existence. With the column, Cunningham is exhibiting architecture in absolute terms, as only itself—pure form without function; the column supports nothing. All his buildings exhibit Cunningham's trust in architecture's own language—whether the celebration of constituent elements like piers and walls, or its basic geometry—and the indisputable power of their presence in Cunningham's buildings, qua architecture, derives from bold, inventive, and unapologetic use of language as form.

But the term "absolute architecture" understates the complexity of Cunningham's work. His single column may declare the autonomy of architecture as a discipline, but Cunningham, in Harmony and all his other buildings, uses the formalism to cultivate many other aspects of the environment and commission, including the sensibility of his buildings' occupants. Form is an instrument, not an end in itself. It is the violin that makes the music possible.

Still, he starts with the instrument, with that column as

Opposite, far left: *Harmony, 1997.* Opposite center: *Razor Bluff, 1998.* Opposite right: *Crescent, 1998, passage from master bedroom to bath.* Previous pages: *Lakehouse, 1986.*

a thing in itself, with its potential to establish its own presence and individuality. In a sense, his interest in nature is a defense against the industrialized, suburbanized building culture that has homogenized the domestic landscape from coast to coast. Like most architects influenced more by Wright than by European Modernists, Cunningham espouses nature rather than the machine because the machine is repetitive in its essence, and therefore standardizing and, as Schindler said, dehumanizing. All angles to Cunningham are valid, as are curvilinear forms, whether derived from the compass or avian imagery.

Like Cunningham himself, his geometries resist typecasting; he avails himself of a wide range with little repetition. But whether they are the minimalist incremental geometries of Cityhouse, the sliding Möbius strips of Seascape, the more recent fractal geometry of Voler or even the structural matrix of the Museum for Japanese Art and Culture, they have common characteristics. As an architect who resolutely breaks the box, Cunningham always opens form. He often lifts the roof off its walls, dissociating their respective geometries by the height of a clerestory. Rarely does he close a design around a bilaterally symmetrical plan or control a house with an authoritarian axis that prescribes or overdetermines the design. He believes in cultivating zones of spatial ambiguity, including a strongly reciprocal relationship between outside and inside: The geometries usually resist the either/or closure of a regular solid. He also believes that buildings should not be understood at first glance, but only through a promenade of discovery.

The geometries, then, are seldom static, and in their movement, they prompt the exploratory promenade. The

stepped planes of Cityhouse, all orthogonal, nonetheless establish a diagonal circulation pattern. The rotational geometries of Wing House spin the eye and body into the landscape. He pivots the entry in Earth Water Fire on a cynlinder. The sense of movement tends to physicalize the architecture, making it experiential. Brandys' critique of Cunningham's dependency on geometry is not entirely accurate, because Cunningham does not use geometry as a tool of control but of release and affinity to a larger environment. In Crescent, the circles and angles draw visitors into and through the house, and finally project their eye out to the view of infinity's beach.

Closed forms like the walls around a medieval city or the shape of a New England saltbox house are usually defensive, whether against the enemy or the weather. Open forms tend to be more receptive to outside forces,

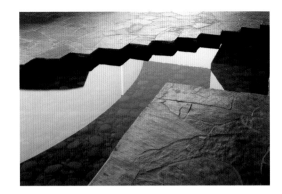

and in Cunningham's buildings, they are actively invitational. His open forms open not only to the landscape but also to the environment in its broadest elemental sense—to the light and to water, especially, but also to the sunsets, the amplitude of Western space, to views, and to all the other positive features of the landscape that Americans, as spiri-

Opposite far left: *Harmony; 1997, reflection in south pool; a garden for the water in your mind.* Opposite center: *Wing House I & II; 1997, 1999.* Opposite right, above, and below (three photos): *Crescent, 1998, terrace, pool, and ramp.* Above left: *Earth Fire Water; 1997, entry pool with reflection.*

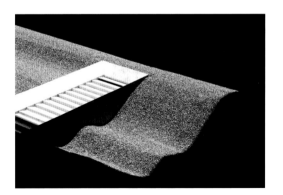

tual heirs to Jefferson, value. It is with and through form that Cunningham cultivates the elements. Cityhouse, Chapel, and the private car and art museum were all designed to operate as venetian blinds, admitting patterns of light in ways that transform the interiors graphically. The clerestories in Aperture allow light to penetrate into the depths of the structure, as though from hidden sources. Cunningham suppresses the edges of his pools, creating "infinity lips" that, because of the absence of a containing frame, are more open to the elements, heightening the effect of reflections and plays of wind across the surface.

But Cunningham does not simply cultivate the elements as a picture. He invites them into the house as phenomena, aware that they transpire in time. He is not interested in the theatrics of lighting and excursions into the visually hyper environments by scenographic artists like Robert Wilson, whose work is literally staged. Phenomena of nature are characterized by change, and as ephemera, they change the building unpredictably, so that it, too, transpires over time. The structure that cultivates phenomena lives in a moment heightened by its transitory nature, in what Cunningham calls "the blush of light" crossing a wall or the breezes that flow, for example, through the enclosed gardens and rooms that alternate in The Arbors. In Cityhouse, the walls when seen frontally form an opaque enclosure, but seen on end, they become transparent and offer long perspectival views: Walking through the house is tantamount to opening and closing shutters. The house takes on an aspect of phenomenal change activated simply by movement.

Cunningham explains the importance of the environmental moment that an object like a house can capture in terms of a vase he passes in his living room every day.

Though it is beautiful, habit has made it invisible: He no longer sees it because it is always there. "But one morning, after three days of gloomy weather, light struck the vase, which happened to be full of water for a bouquet of leaves that my wife, Pamela, had arranged. From one angle, it was magic: The leaves were backlit. I looked for my camera."

Cunningham designs his houses and museums to look for the shadows, the reflections, the bouncing light—for the phenomena that make the ordinary physical world momentarily extraordinary because of a transformative effect. If his houses are not ideated by concept and theory, they are phenomenalized: Experience itself is the concept and theory. A few years after his first projects, Cunningham started designing large pools of water with borderless rims that both blend into and mirror the sky while reflecting shimmering patterns onto surrounding surfaces. "When you're dealing with water, you're designing

only half of something. The reflection completes the other half. There's incredible patterning and glistening. The edges of water are a special opportunity, because that's where you can make the water appear to float. It stops you. You meditate. Maybe you even wonder." He gardens the elements, intensifying nature as the sum of its phenomena, transforming houses from objects into experience fields verging on environmental art.

By the nature of his search, Cunningham does not try to control the phenomena so much as create the conditions that can set them off. Impregnated with an ephemer-

Opposite left: *Outlook; 1997.* Opposite right: *Canyon House; 2000.* Above left: *Wave, 1987.* Above: *Spindrift; 2004, construction is currently scheduled to commence in 2006.*

al effect, the inert object, even at the scale of a museum like Museum for Japanese Art and Culture, takes on a life of its own as it becomes phenomenal. Cunningham prefers to spend his attention and budget on bringing natural effects into his structures rather than lavishing expensive materials on the surfaces. A plain, smooth-troweled wall registers washes of light better than anigré paneling. He uses fine stones not for their pictorial textures but for their reflective qualities. He prefers plays of immateriality to displays of materiality. "It's unfortunate when a building is a stage set and things are padded to give the appearance of stability and permanence," he says. "The interior is hollow."

Deploying all the formal and organizational means at

Left: *Mist in the Pines, 2003.* Below left: *Ocean Steps, 1999.* Below center: *Cadence, 1998.* Below: *Rising Sun, 1988.*

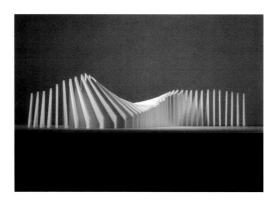

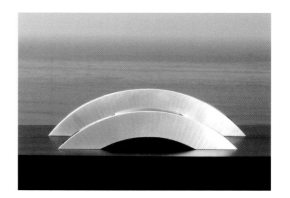

an architect's disposal to invite plays of light, space, and elemental phenomena into his architecture, Cunningham creates sense baths, highly immersive environments aimed at sensuous rather than ideated pleasures. This is architecture meant for the skin and the eye, though it is not merely tactile. Cunningham orchestrates a shift in emphasis from object to subject, from the building as a static thing, to the building as a catalyst and receptacle for ephemera: The buildings are most powerful when the elemental physics of the environment act on the occupant. The building is not clinically detached from the viewer but interactive, a lens for seeing and a conduit for channeling and provoking sensation. The buildings exist somewhere in the vibration

Right: *Arabesque; 2004.* Below: *Outlook; 1997.* Below right: *Arabesque; 2004.* Below far right:: *Cascade, 2006.*

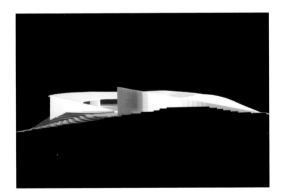

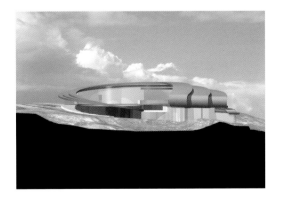

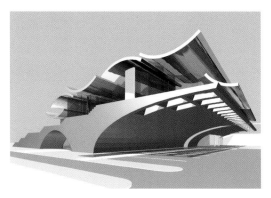

you can walk up to and feel something you've never felt before," he says. "Buildings need to radiate emotion."

Cunningham admires the ethereal illusions of light-and-space artists such as Robert Irwin and James Turrell. Like these artists, Cunningham aspires to an architecture intended to provoke forms of wonder. As a San Diego architect, Cunningham is especially cognizant of Louis Kahn's Salk Institute: "There's no other feeling quite like standing in the courtyard of the Salk Institute. It absolutely communicates absolutely."

In his travels, he has found architecture that supports his ideal of an environmental mysticism. Michelucci, the postwar Italian Modernist, was an expressionist who focused with equal intensity and skill on concrete and shadow. "There's an agony in his buildings. La chiesa dell'Autostrada captures an astonishing feeling: It's primarily emotional, not rational." Cunningham also finds that certain works by Carlo Scarpa have an auratic quality, sustained by his impeccable detailing, the craft, and the exquisite materiality. Both Italians are architects who design with deliberate specificity, creating unique spatial moments in which light figures mysteriously. "Buildings need to radiate feelings and emotions. They're not just visual," he says. "I always try to achieve an unseen quality beyond physical appearance." He agrees, then, with Marcel Duchamp that art has become too retinal, but while Duchamp cultivated

between form and phenomena, each cultivating the other. The house engages the occupant in interactivity: The space of the house and the space of the occupant overlap in a field of experience.

Though his forms are abstract, he shifts from the Modernist belief in objectivity toward a belief in the power of environments designed to elicit subjective responses. Cunningham elicits emotions by engaging the senses. "Buildings are not just visual. I want buildings that a more conceptual approach, Cunningham ultimately and ideally seeks aura. He dismisses architecture that, in its clarity, is too knowable. "I always strive not just for the physical aspects of a design, but for this unseen quality," he says. "Is it going to make you feel something, like the Salk? You want that inner feeling that gives you a sense of place that you can't get anywhere else. It's not just churches that can deliver a religious experience."

Curiously, Cunningham often succeeds in eliciting these feelings in small rooms, such as the enclosed powder room of Promontory, in focused settings with just a few materials and spatial moves. Frequently he encloses the room completely, allowing light to fall only from above in a gentle gradient on smooth, pure walls that have no seams, few changes of materials, and muted contrasts of color. The powder rooms seem like chapels, with light coming from above and solid stone washbasins carved and detailed with the care and gravity of sacramental fonts. "I don't think that just the church should offer a spatial experience that touches the soul."

After more than a quarter of a century of practice, Cunningham knows exactly the kind of architecture he is striving to conceive, and in that time, he has also acquired the technical expertise to achieve it. In an Irwin scrim installation, the gauzy effects are dependent on the minimal connection between the fabric and the frame. In a Turrell, the opaque surround must taper to a thin line so that its lack of dimensionality, the immateriality of the surround, defers to the light and allows it to pulse.

Spaces of wonder require a special insight and the expertise of a virtuoso artisan. Cunningham has mastered the craft of materializing the immaterial.

Opposite top and bottom: *Las Terrazas; 2007.*
Below: Leaves in the Wind, 2006.
Following Pages, from left to right: *Razor Bluff; 1998; Razor Bluff; detail of stair through light and shadow; Harmony, 1997, terrace fireplace; Crescent; 1998, living room fireplace, gas in shattered glass. Reflection has always been an important element in Cunningham's designs. In each of these photos, Cunningham has created reflections that free the structures from the ground and turn them into floating objects. "You can look down and see the sky at your feet," he says. "One can judge the hour of the day from the way turning shadows projected by the sun register on the building as on the face of a sundial, connecting the dimension of time. The shadows, along with the reflected images, are an ethereal text scripted on buildings that remind us, poetically, of important intangibles."*

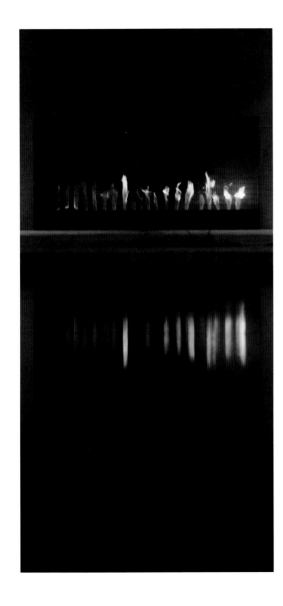

PROJECTS (dates refer to year the project was begun)

CURRENT PROJECTS IN DESIGN
RESIDENCE, 2006, Pebble Beach, CA.
RESIDENCE, 2006, Aurezza Monterrey, Mexico.
FIVE RESIDENCES, 2006, La Jolla, CA.
UNIVERSITY HOUSE, 2006, La Jolla, CA.
SPINDRIFT, 2006, Point Loma, CA.
TWO RESIDENCES, 2004, Rancho Santa Fe, CA.
THE MUSEUM FOR JAPANESE ART & CULTURE, 2004, Hanford, CA.
RESIDENCE, 2003, San Diego, CA.
VOLER, 1999, Lake Hodges, CA.

CURRENT PROJECTS IN CONSTRUCTION
VELOCITY, 2001, Tucson, AZ.
RAZOR BLUFF, 1998, La Jolla, CA.

SELECTED COMPLETED PROJECTS
RAY, 1999, La Jolla, CA.
WING HOUSE II, 1999, Rancho Santa Fe, CA.
THE BOX HOUSE, 1993, Rancho Santa Fe, CA.
CRESCENT, 1998, Leucadia, CA.
HARMONY, 1997, Rancho Santa Fe, CA.
ARBORS, 1997, Rancho Santa Fe, CA.
EARTH FIRE WATER, 1997, Rancho Santa Fe, CA.
PROMONTORY, 1997, Rancho Santa Fe, CA.
BRUSHSTROKE., 1995, La Jolla, CA.
CITYHOUSE, 1995, La Jolla, CA.
LAKE HOUSE, 1986, Escondido, CA.
APERTURE, 1986, Del Dios, CA.
SEA VIEW, 1985, San Clemente, CA.
CABIN, 1985, Pine Hills, Julian, CA.
WING HOUSE I, 1979, Rancho Santa Fe, CA.
FOX VALLEY PARK DISTRICT NATURE CENTER, Deck and Exhibits. 1975–1976. Aurora, IL.

PUBLICATIONS (Selected)

BOOKS

Organic Architecture: The Other Modernism. Alan Hess. 2006.

Art Invention House. Michael Webb. November 2005.

1000 Architects. The Images Publishing Group Pty Ltd. 2004.

Brave New Houses. Michael Webb. October 2003.

AIA Guidebook. Dirk Sutro. January 2003.

Houses of the World (German, French, and Spanish Editions). Francisco Arsenio Cerver. 2000.

Casas de Alta Montaña. Oscar Asensio. 2000.

Hyperwest: American Residential Architecture on the Edge. Alan Hess. 1996.

A Taliesin Legacy. Tobias Guggenheimer. 1995.

The Los Angeles House. Timothy Street-Porter. 1995.

West Coast Wave.. Dirk Sutro. New York. 1994.

NEWSPAPERS AND JOURNALS

San Diego Union Tribune. Bell. "What's Haut?" November 21, 2002.

San Diego Union Tribune. James. "At Home in California." November 17, 2002.

San Diego Business Journal. Horn. "Architect-Designed Homes Attract Sophisticated Buyers." May 2002.

San Diego Union Tribune. Jarmusch. "Magazine goes Ga-Ga over Cunningham's Design." April 23, 2000.

Los Angeles Times. Epstein. "Amid South County's Tracts, Some Gems of Architecture." December 1998.

Journal of Taliesin Fellows. Van Doren. Issue 19. Spring 1996.

San Diego Union Tribune. Jarmusch. "House of Light." January 8, 1995.

Journal of Taliesin Fellows. Wiehle. Issues 13-14. Summer 1994.

San Diego Union Tribune. Jarmusch. "S.D. Architecture Shines in Book." December 12, 1993.

Journal of Taliesin Fellows. Sweeney. Issue 6. Spring 1992.

La Jolla Light. Keller. "An Art Perspective From an Architect's View." July 1991.

San Diego Union Tribune. Olton. "Energized Dreams." July 14, 1991.

Athenaeum Newsletter. "Architecture As Art." July 1991.

San Diego Union. Jarmusch. "Architect Won't Let Conventional Plans Box Him." April 19, 1991.

Los Angeles Times. Sutro. "A Jewel-Like Exhibit." April 18, 1991.

San Diego Union Tribune. Jarmusch. "Be Bolder, Local Architects Urged." October 23, 1990.

1988 Greater San Diego Chamber of Commerce Housing Guide. Sutro. Westward Press. 1988.

The Tribune. Riddle. "Master's Shadow Still Influences Industry." Copley Press. November 13, 1987.

San Diego Tribune.. Morgan. "Design Lines." September 1987.

Los Angeles Times. "Ray: A Dream House is Built Around a Spectacular View." January 27, 1986.

The Citizen. Wilson. "Putting the Pieces Together." South Coast Newspapers. January 22, 1986.

Los Angeles Times. Kaplan. "Schindler House Exhibition". Los Angeles Times. January 19, 1986.

San Diego Union. Kaiser. "Work of Art – A Building on the Cliffs." Copley Press. November 10, 1985.

San Diego Union. Kaiser. "Architects Aim for Natural Look." Copley Press. May 19, 1985.

Los Angeles Times Home Magazine.. Kaplan. "Duo of Distinction." February 17, 1985.

San Diego Union. Sutter. The Santa Fe Chamber Music Society. July 11, 1982.

The Beacon News. "Parks." "Gridley House: Beauty, Truth, History." "Goin' Fish-in." "Scenic River View." "All You Have to Do is Look Up." (Family Leisure-Magazine Section). "Log Cabin." "When is a House More Than a Home?" Aurora: Copley Press. 1974. 1975. 1979. 1981. 1982.

MAGAZINES

Global Architecture Houses 92. Projects 2006.

Architectural Digest. Haldeman. "California Reflections. A Scuptural La Jolla Residence Strikes a Balance Between Yin and Yang. January 2006.

Global Architecture Houses 86. Projects 2005.

Architectural Digest. Giovannini. "A World Apart near San Diego." April 2005.

The Robb Report. Brooks. "Ultimate Home Tour." April 2005.

P R O J E C T S , P U B L I C A T I O N S

Riviera. Francis. "A Few Minutes With." March 2005.

Architectural Digest. von Hoffman. "The Professionals: Wallace E. Cunningham, Exploring the Personal Nature of Architecture with Houses That Stir the Soul." December 2004.

Luxury Living. Graham. "Coastal Jewel." Fall 2004.

San Diego Magazine. Shess. "Master of Light. The Illuminating Architecture of Wallace Cunningham." July 2004.

San Diego Home/Garden. Manson. "San Diego Issues." April 2004.

Architectural Digest. "The AD 100. Architectural Digest's International Directory of Interior Designers and Architects." January 2004.

San Diego Magazine. "Designing for the Soul. One Man's Definition of Design." January 2004.

Architectural Digest. AD Style. "Great Design Under $100." December 2003.

Architectural Digest. "Designers Discover Design." November 2003.

Architectural Digest. Giovannini. "Framing Device." October 2003.

San Diego Home/Garden. Manson. "Lost in Space. The Unsung Architecture of San Diego." May 2003.

Architectural Digest– Russian. Giovannini. "Spinning the Senses." March 2003.

Architectural Digest—Spanish. Giovannini. "Spinning the Senses." February 2003.

Architectural Digest. Giovannini. "Spinning the Senses." December 2002.

San Diego Home/Garden. San Diego Life. Geography Lesson. July 2002.

Global Architecture Houses 70. Projects 2002.

San Diego Home/Garden. San Diego Life. Master Designer. December 2001.

Wallpaper. Design Directory 2001. July/August 2001.

San Diego Home/Garden. Manson. "Drawing the Battle Lines." May 2001. "Readers Respond." July 2001.

Arcade. Monsen. "The Houses of Wallace Cunningham." Spring 2001.

Global Architecture Houses 63. Projects 2000.

San Diego Home/Garden. "In Focus." Twentieth Anniversary Edition. August 1999.

Mercedes Momentum. Ostrow. "Kitchen Sync - Design Ideas That Fit Your Dreams." Summer 1999.

San Diego Magazine. Foster Residence Pool. June 1999.

San Diego Home/Garden. Foster Residence Pool. Pool Awards. June 1999.

Decor & Style. Wolff. "Requa Rediscovered"- San Diego Architect Created Southern California Style. December 1998.

San Diego Home/Garden. April 1998.

Decor & Style. April 1998.

Global Architecture Houses 55. Projects 1998.

Decors, France. Issue Sept./Oct./Nov. 1997.

Global Architecture Houses 52. Projects 1997.

San Diego Home/Garden. Art/Design News. September 1997.

Hauser Prohl. "Durch glas zum lichte." February 1996.

Global Architecture Houses 48. Projects 1996.

House Beautiful. Zevon. "Meeting the Challenge." February 1995.

San Diego Home/Garden. Sutro. "Lifestyles. Fifteenth Anniversary." September 1994.

San Diego Home/Garden. Van Doren. Art & Design. July 1994.

Global Architecture Houses 92. WALLY: IS THIS CORRECT?

Projects 2006

Los Angeles Times Magazine. Hess. "Style Rooms With Many Views." October 1997.

Global Architecture Houses 31. Projects 1991.

Los Angeles Times. Sutro. "Cunningham's Uncanny Sense of Spirituality." September 13, 1990.

San Diego Magazine. Terpening. "A Sculpture in the Sun." May 1990.

San Diego Home/Garden. Van Doren. "Aperture." April 1989.

Ranch & Coast. Clark. "The Shape of Homes to Come." January 1988.

San Diego Home/Garden. Van Doren. "Arc in the Pines." Westward Press. December 1987.

Cartouche. Prouvedini. "Design as Dance." New School of Architecture, San Diego. Spring 1988.

The Citizen. Wilson. "Homes That Are Truly Original Spaces." November 26, 1986.

KPBS On-Air Magazine. Van Doren. "Building the San Diego Dream." March 1986.

Architecture and Urbanism. Nakaura. "Wallace E. Cunningham." Tokyo. March 1985.

San Diego Home/Garden. Jensen. "A Leaf Falls." Westward Press. November 1982.

TELEVISION & RADIO

HGTV. Nancy Glass Productions. "Top 10 Most Amazing Homes" Wing House. August 2003.

"The Lounge" KPBS Radio. Sutro. "Architecture as it Relates to Music & Art." August 2003.

"The Lounge" KPBS Radio. Sutro. The Influence of Japanese Culture on American Architecture. March & July 2003.

"Talk With Tricia" San Diego Home/Garden Radio Show, KCBQ 1170 AM, February 3, 2002.

KGTB Channel 10. McBride. "Graycliff" (Aperture). McGraw-Hill Broadcasting. February 3, 1986.

WLS Channel 7, Chicago. "C.B. & Q. Roundhouse: Saved From Demolition." 1976.

EXHIBITS, LECTURES AND TOURS

GA Gallery (Global Architecture). Exhibit. Tokyo, Japan. March 25 through May 21, 2006.

Santa Ana College Art Forum. Lecture. Contemporary Issues in Art & Architecture. September 2003.

GA Gallery (Global Architecture). Exhibit. Tokyo, Japan. April 20 through July 2, 2002.

"Rock Paper Scissors" - An Exhibition of Architectural Art. Flux Gallery, San Diego, CA. January 12 through February 23, 2001.

GA Gallery (Global Architecture). Exhibit. Tokyo, Japan. March 11 through April 9, 2000.

American Institute of Architecture (AIA). Lecture. Del Mar, CA. May 26, 1999.

Taliesin West. Lecture. Taliesin Apprentice Lecture Series. Scottsdale, AZ. March 5, 1999.

San Bernardino Valley College. KVCR TV Taping. San Bernardino, CA. December 15, 1998.

Museum of Architecture. Exhibit & Lecture. "Houses" San Juan Capistrano, CA. November 1998 through January 1999.

University of California at San Diego. Exhibition and Tour. "Eight on the Edge." April 24, 1998.

Society of Architectural Historians, 1998.

L.A. Museum of Contemporary Art, 1998.

Mesa College Catalog. Sweeney. "Wallace E. Cunningham." April 1992.

The Schindler House. Exhibit. Hollywood, CA. November 8, 1991 through February 9, 1992.

Athenaeum. Exhibit. "Architecture as Art." La Jolla, CA. July 2, 1991.

Athenaeum. Lecture. Music and Arts Library. La Jolla, CA. July 19, 1991.

San Diego Mesa College. Exhibit. Mesa College Art Gallery. May 8 through August 8, 1991.

San Diego Mesa College. Lecture. "Environmental Design and Theory." San Diego, CA. May 7, 1991.

San Diego Mesa College Home Tours for Vocational Class. San Diego, CA. October 10, 1990.

San Diego Museum of Art. Gallery Talk. "Capturing the Spirit of the Age." August 16, 1990.

Gamble House. Lecture. Pasadena, CA. May 3, 1990.

University of California San Diego. Lecture. April 7, 1989.

New School of Architecture. Architectural Lecture Series. San Diego, CA. May 13, 1988.

New School of Architecture. Exhibit. San Diego, CA. October 16, 1987.

San Diego 9. Wadkins. New School of Architecture, San Diego, CA . 1987.

La Jolla Women's Club. Exhibit. La Jolla, CA. April 10, 1986.

The Schindler House. "Thrive." Hollywood, CA. January 10 through March 8, 1986.

International Gallery. "Architecture: Continuing Dialogue." San Diego, CA. November 5, 1985.

Pierce College. "Works of Innovation in Architecture." Thousands Oaks, CA. February 20, 1985.

San Diego State University. Lecture. "My Work." May 17, 1984.

La Jolla Chamber Music Society. Tour. "Wing House." Rancho Santa Fe, CA. June 1982.

HONORS

International Academy of Architecture. Special Prize in the EXHIBITION-COMPETITION OF ARCHITECTURAL PROJECTS AND BUILT WORKS – Interarch 2003.

Opposite: *Velocity, 2001, a writers' retreat in Arizona.*
Page 160: *Shadow and light at Crescent.*

INDEX

Entries that refer to photographs are in *italics*; the main entry for each house is in **bold.**